NEW YORK METROPOLITAN REGION STUDY

RAYMOND VERNON, DIRECTOR

A STUDY UNDERTAKEN BY THE GRADUATE

SCHOOL OF PUBLIC ADMINISTRATION,

HARVARD UNIVERSITY, FOR

REGIONAL PLAN ASSOCIATION, INC.

Max Hall, Editorial Director

WAGES IN THE METROPOLIS

THEIR INFLUENCE ON THE LOCATION OF INDUSTRIES IN THE NEW YORK REGION

By Martin Segal

HARVARD UNIVERSITY PRESS
Cambridge, Massachusetts · 1960

Endpaper map by Jeanyee Wong

Designed by Marcia R. Lambrecht

Library of Congress Catalog Card Number 60–5396
Printed in the United States of America

Foreword

This is one of a series of books on the forces that shape metropolitan areas. In particular, the series has to do with the forces that shape the largest and most complex metropolitan area in the United States, a 22-county expanse which takes in parts of three states but which, for convenience, we term the New York Metropolitan Region.

In 1956, the Regional Plan Association, a nonprofit research and planning agency whose purpose is to promote the coordinated development of these 22 counties, requested the Graduate School of Public Administration of Harvard University to undertake a three-year study of the Region. The challenging task was to analyze the key economic and demographic features of the Region and to project them to 1965, 1975, and 1985.

The resulting studies are reports to the Regional Plan Association. At the same time, they are designed to be of service to a much broader audience. Most Americans now live in metropolitan areas; indeed ever-increasing proportions of the world's populations are gravitating to metropolitan clusters. Their well-being depends to a considerable extent on how these areas develop. Yet the scholar's understanding of the currents underlying the rise of such areas seems grossly inadequate.

As a study of these underlying currents, this project is neither a blueprint for action nor an analysis of metropolitan government. It has no recommendations to make about the physical structure of the Region or about the form or activities of the governmental bodies there. At the same time, it is a necessary prelude to future planning studies of the Region and to well considered recommendations for governmental action. Its end product is an analysis of the Region's probable development, assuming that the economic and demographic forces in sight follow their indicated course and assuming that the role of government is largely limited to existing policies.

The results of the Study, it is hoped, will be applied in many ways. Governments and enterprises in the Region should be in a better position to plan their future programs if they become more closely aware of the economic environment in which they may expect to operate. Other metropolitan areas, it is already evident, will benefit from the methodology and conclusions the Study has developed.

From the first, there has been a general recognition that the main part of the Study would have to be done by a group located within the New York Metropolitan Region and devoted exclusively to the project. Such a group was assembled in New York. The work that followed was a complex partnership. The New York staff functioned in close harness with members of the Harvard University faculty. It drew on the faculties of other universities, including Columbia University, Fordham University, Hofstra College, New York University, and Rutgers University. It obtained the help of dozens of governmental organizations in the Region, and literally hundreds of private groups and individuals. It made use of the materials which the Regional Plan Association had pulled together in prior years.

Each book in the series has a place in the total structure of the Study; yet each is designed to be a complete work in itself. The final report, containing the synthesis and projections of the Study, is scheduled for publication sometime in 1960.

It is not easy to account for all the elements that went into the making of this book nor of the others in the series. The Regional Plan Association performed an indispensable function in conceiving and sponsoring the idea of a study. The Ford Foundation and the Rockefeller Brothers Fund generously provided the financial support. The usual formula in such a situation obviously applies: credit for the Study's results must be shared with those who helped to bring it about, but the onus of error or omission lies with us.

The several volumes in the series bear the names of their principal authors. The undertaking as a whole has been under the direction of Raymond Vernon. He is responsible for the final report and parts of other studies, and his guidance is evident throughout the series.

Edward S. Mason
for the Graduate School of Public
Administration, Harvard University

Contents

Tables

I

Wages and Skills as Locational Factors

This is a book with a difficult mission. What we hope to achieve between its two covers is principally to give the reader an understanding of the part that wage levels have played in conditioning the location of industries in the New York Metropolitan Region, and what part the wage factor may yet play in the future. We shall have a secondary objective, too—that of indicating the part which labor skills have played in maintaining the New York area's advantage.

But wages and skills, as we shall see, interact in a very complex way with other locational forces—with transportation, for example, and with various factors of a less familiar sort—in imposing their influence on an area like New York. So we are bound to introduce these other forces as well, in order to make the comparative importance of wages and skills amply clear. There is this distinction, however. We have sought to document all that is documentable about wages and to present our argument with respect to the role of skills, but our discussion of the other factors is offered *ex cathedra,* as a distillation of conclusions developed more fully in other volumes of the New York Metropolitan Region Study. The reader whose prime concern is with our findings on the subject of wages and skills, therefore, should find all of the relevant argument within this volume. But the reader who must be "shown" concerning every side of the locational problem will want to pursue the argument contained in other volumes.

The New York Metropolitan Region embraces the five boroughs of New York City and the seventeen counties clustered around it. All told, the Region covers nearly seven thousand square miles, stretching from the eastern tip of Long Island almost to the western boundary of New Jersey, and from the northern reaches of New York's Dutchess County down to Monmouth County on the Jersey coast. Within this area thousands of factories, shops, and offices—as well as some garrets and historic farmhouses—provide places of work for about seven million men and women, a labor force larger than that of many a European country.

In some ways, this huge labor market * does not seem to differ from the rest of the nation's urban economy. To be sure, the rate of labor-force participation of young white women and of Negro women of all ages is somewhat higher than elsewhere; but this difference is not very great. A larger proportion of the male labor force is occupied in managerial and clerical jobs than in most other metropolitan areas, and a larger proportion of the female labor force falls in the category of semiskilled mechanical workers—the so-called operatives. Yet even these differences are not striking.

But as we take a close look at the Region's industries, we begin to perceive marked differences from other urban areas. An examination of statistics in Table 1, for instance, suggests some of the special features of the nonmanufacturing sector: the relatively high concentration of business-service establishments, of financial institutions, and of wholesaling units—a large proportion of each extending their services to customers and clients beyond the limits of the Region. For example, the Region, with less than 10 per cent of the nation's population, possesses 20 per cent of its financial and real estate em-

* The precise definition of "labor market" raises many theoretical questions which cannot be considered here. Most economists would probably agree that in one sense, at least, a labor market is a concentration of economic activity in which enough job opportunities exist to permit most workers to change employment without changing residence. The New York Metropolitan Region contains, in effect, a number of interconnected and overlapping labor markets, but they are subject to common wage-determining forces and can be considered for our purposes as a single labor market.

Table 1 Employment in New York Metropolitan Region by Types of Industries, 1956

	Number of employees (thousands)	As percentage of U. S. employment
Total employment	6,699.8	10.4
Manufacturing and ordnance	1,889.9	11.6
Wholesale trade	453.5	14.9
Finance and real estate	466.8	20.1
Business services [a]	358.6	22.0
Public utilities	460.5	11.7
Retail trade	750.8	9.8
Personal and "mixed" [b] services	548.2	11.0
Construction	241.8	9.5
Agriculture [c]	45.3	1.9
All other [d]	1,484.4	7.5

[a] Includes the employees in central administrative offices of manufacturing, mining, and retail enterprises. Similar employees in wholesale trade are included in "wholesale trade."

[b] Industries in which neither personal nor business services are clearly predominant. Includes professional and nonprofit organizations.

[c] Includes forestry, fishing, mining, and agricultural services. Note that agricultural employment, like the categories above it on the list, does not include the self-employed. See note d.

[d] Government, self-employed, and domestic workers. The employment figure of 1,484,400 includes about 11,600 employees of foreign governments and international bodies, but these were subtracted before the 7.5 per cent was computed, because the available national total did not include such employees.

Sources: Estimates of the New York Metropolitan Region Study based on U. S. Bureau of the Census, *County Business Patterns, First Quarter 1956;* and on data obtained from the state departments of labor of New York, New Jersey, and Connecticut and from federal Bureau of Old-Age and Survivors Insurance.

ployment. The very nature of these business, financial, and wholesale institutions suggests the wide variety of specialized skills characterizing the Region's labor force, a variety not revealed in the broad occupational categories of the Bureau of the Census.

But equally striking is the composition of the manufacturing sector. Though covering only 11.6 per cent of the nation's employment in that category, the manufacturing sector illustrates both the uniqueness and the complexity of the Region's economy.

The Region has a greater number of manufacturing industries than any other metropolitan area. Of the 450 classifications into which the federal government divides United States industry, only 35 or 40 are lacking in the New York Metropolitan Region, and those are primarily industries whose location is tied to the source of raw materials. Another distinguishing characteristic of the Region's manufacturing is the relative importance of consumer-goods industries which sell their products in national markets. Forty per cent of its manufacturing employment falls in this category; except for Detroit, whose automobile manufacture gives it special prominence as a producer of consumer goods, this is the highest proportion found in any major metropolitan area.

Even within the category of national-market consumer goods, the Region specializes in particular kinds of industries. These are industries in which an overwhelming proportion of firms have only one plant and in which the plants are especially small—typically employing less than 50 workers. The products manufactured by these industries span the whole spectrum of apparel, from the most expensive dresses to casual slippers; they include also a variety of other products, such as jewelry, toys, sporting goods, pens and pencils.

In addition to goods for the consumer, the Region's plants turn out an assortment of "intermediate products" used by other producers. And in many such industries, including printing machinery, elevators, electrical instruments, and medicinal chemicals for food producers, the Region contains a relatively high share of the nation's employment and "exports" much of the output to markets beyond its own area. In contrast with the establishments in most consumer-goods industries, the plants in the industries making intermediate products are large and generally belong to firms which also have plants outside the New York Metropolitan Region.

The point we propose to develop in this chapter is that, *at any moment in time,* most of the jobs contained within the New York

Metropolitan Region are quite impervious to the lure of other areas, so far as wages and skills are concerned; stated differently, neither a relative improvement nor a relative decline in the area's wage or skill characteristics could have much locational effect on most of its economic activity. The sector whose location in the Region is acutely sensitive to differences in wages or to differences in the supply of skills, as between one geographical area and another, is quite small.

Still, the wage and skill factors are of considerable importance in explaining the area's past development and projecting its future. They are important partly because segments of the nation's industries are continually becoming sensitive to wage and skill differences. This sensitivity, as we shall see, may be the result of any one of several developments, notably such things as changes in the technology of either production or transportation, or changes in the nature of the products. Such segments, once they become sensitive, often react quickly to regional differences in wages and skills.

This is why, *at any point in time,* it is so hard to find many jobs under serious pressure in an area like the New York Metropolitan Region, and why it is so misleading to infer from such an observation that the wage and skill issues are of little importance. Ten or twenty years ago, there were jobs in the Region, operating under heavy external wage pressure, which now are no longer there. A decade or two hence, many jobs which now seem invulnerable to such pressure may well have moved into the wage-sensitive category.

LABOR COSTS AND LOCATIONAL CALCULUS

The location of individual firms in a particular area is not always a result of rational economic considerations. Many firms select locations because of personal preferences of managers and owners. Many firms pursue their activity without even asking themselves: Why are we here? Can we do better in some other location? But when a firm's locational choice is flatly inconsistent with the calculus of economic advantage, it is likely to find its existence threatened by more favorably located competitors; the competitors will grow at the expense of the poorly located firm. As a result, the locational distribution of broad groups of firms does adhere to a certain rational pattern which may seem absent from the decisions of particular firms.

What is the nature of the influence which labor markets exert on such locational patterns? Any management that makes even a superficial attempt to survey a number of potential locations will observe that areas differ with respect to the prevailing wage levels, the size of the local supply of skilled labor, the extent of collective bargaining, and even at times the efficiency of the local workers. These differences add up to differences in labor costs per unit of output. Hence, by considering the labor-market characteristics of alternative locations, a firm may be able to reduce its total cost of operation.

Expenditures on labor are a very large item in the cost structure of most businesses. Thus, in manufacturing as a whole, labor costs are roughly 15 times as large as space costs and 21 times as large as local and state taxes.[1] Furthermore, the characteristics of labor markets which influence labor costs differ widely among various geographical areas. For example, unskilled workers engaged in manufacturing in New Orleans are paid about 30 per cent less, on the average, than similar workers in New York. Since labor costs are so big and so different among areas, it might appear that such costs would be a predominant factor in the locational calculus of business firms. And yet, we have concluded that most firms in the New York area are comparatively invulnerable to labor-cost differences in their locational decisions. What is the explanation?

In general terms the explanation is simply that the size of labor costs is only one of many factors affecting the competitive position of the Region's firms. This position is also influenced by other costs: costs of transporting raw materials or finished products, costs of subcontracting work to other firms, costs of power and of other items. Moreover, the profitability of these enterprises is also affected by their ability to provide quick customer service or to maintain close contacts with suppliers. Many firms in the Region could easily find other geographical areas in which they could conduct their business with lower labor costs per unit of output. But location in such areas might increase their costs outside the field of labor, or reduce opportunities for easy contact with suppliers or customers. The magnitude of these handicaps could offset any potential savings in labor costs. In some cases, the increase in nonlabor costs, such as freight, would be greater than the reduction in the costs of labor; in other cases, the decrease in demand for the firm's product would reduce the firm's profitability despite the possible reduction in labor costs. Any firm to which these conditions apply must be classified as insensitive to geographic labor-cost differentials, and thus insensitive in its locational pattern to the conditions of labor markets in particular areas.

Throughout the discussion, however, we must bear in mind what we indicated earlier—that the "insensitivity" of any firm to labor-market conditions is not necessarily a lasting thing. Firms which can afford to ignore labor-cost or skill considerations at one point of time may find such considerations to be the nub of their locational problem a decade later.

One reason for such change lies in technological developments. The improvement of road systems and the development of fast, light trucks, for instance, have reduced the advantages which a textile dyeing and finishing plant once had in being close to the high-style Garment Center in New York City. Manufacturers, therefore, could think of the possibility of abandoning Paterson in the New York Metropolitan Region for a relatively low-wage location in New England. On the other hand, the introduction of labor-saving equipment in the manufacture of medical syringes has had the opposite effect in that industry. By reducing the labor cost of the operation very considerably, the innovations have rendered the industry relatively insensitive to labor-market considerations.

Another factor which has altered the labor sensitivity of some industries has been a change in the nature of the product. The knit outerwear industry, for instance, had once been quite insensitive to style modifications. But, as the design and production of sweaters began to emphasize style, the location of the industry shifted from areas of low labor cost to centers of fashion designing and style leadership. In the men's clothing industry, on the other hand, style changes had an opposite effect. Much of the sportswear and informal "suburban" garments which has been displacing the more traditional types of men's attire is manufactured on a mass-production basis by relatively unskilled labor. The shift to this type of production has increased the labor-cost sensitivity of the industry.

Thus, our classification of the Region's economy in terms of sensitivity to labor-market conditions is clearly not a permanent one. As technology and demand change, they lead to a continual process of locational reorientation, a process which for some industries, or sections of industries, increases the importance of labor-market considerations.

Nor can we insist that any industry which seems relatively insensitive to *moderate* differences in labor costs would remain so for differences more sizable. In the complex economy of the Region there are many borderline cases. But it is still possible to point to a sector of the Region's industries in which, at the present time, wage or skill considerations are a major factor influencing location. Once we identify this sector it will be possible to proceed with the analysis of our central problem—the impact of wages and skills on the Region's economic growth. The sector will emerge more clearly if we first clear out of the way the various large categories of industries that may be called labor-*insensitive.*

THE LABOR-INSENSITIVE ACTIVITIES

✓ The local market

About 59 per cent of the New York Metropolitan Region's labor force is in activities engaged principally in supplying goods and services locally—either to consumers or to other industries. As a whole, these enterprises are relatively invulnerable to outside competition; hence, though they may be dissatisfied in various ways with the Region's labor market, a comparison of the market with other areas will not induce them to change location.

Firms which cater directly to the needs of consumers form an important part of this group. Retail stores; a variety of personal-service establishments ranging from Turkish baths to auto repair shops; a considerable portion of the Region's banks, real estate agencies, and insurance offices; carriers of passengers and goods; public utilities—all these and similar types of business can normally conduct their activity only in the population centers which they serve. To some extent the growth of this "local" sector depends passively upon the growth of other types of economic activity in the New York area. To some extent its own expansion through investment in stores, offices, and service facilities provides a stimulus to the rise in the Region's employment and income. But whatever the factors determining the growth of this sector, its location will be within the general boundaries of the New York Metropolitan Region.

The wage rates of workers in such industries in the Region may—and in fact they do—differ considerably from those in other metropolitan areas or smaller communities through the country.* Even though these differences will not cause the activities to leave the Region, it is important to understand why the differences occur, for the wage levels of "local" industries affect those of the Region's other industries. What is more, wage costs in "local" industries can alter the disposition of the Region's total labor force. An increase in laundry workers' wages, for instance, could lead to an expansion of laundromats and release such workers for use in other industries, such as the garment industries. Therefore, though laundry operators could not seriously consider serving the New York market from an area of lower labor cost, the wages they pay can affect the labor-market conditions of other enterprises which do have such a choice.

Enterprises insulated from outside competition are found not only in the fields of trade and services but also in manufacturing. Breweries, bakeries, bottling works, newspapers, and ice cream producers, for example, are largely limited to the areas they serve. For this group, transport costs suppress effective competition from outside the Region. Products like bread and beer are far bulkier than the ingredients which have to be imported from outside the Region to

* Wage comparisons between the Region and other areas, in these and other industries, are presented in Chapter 3.

make them up. Products like newspapers and ice cream are "perishable," each in its own sense; neither can travel very far without incurring high costs relative to its value.

Another important sector of the Region's economy which is insulated from outside competition is the construction industry. The location of this group is tied closely to the area in which it actually performs its economic service. Though one might consider bringing cheaper work crews from distant locations for local jobs, the cost of transporting and maintaining such labor away from home would usually wipe out any possible gain. Moreover, the pattern of collective bargaining inhibits the use of outside crews. According to the terms of the local contracts, the rates set by the local unions must ordinarily be paid regardless of the source of labor. As a result, the Region's construction industry is largely protected from the competition of firms located in areas of lower labor cost. And, though the rise of prefabricated housing eliminates certain functions previously performed by local labor, this constitutes a relatively minor threat for the present.

Once again, however, we must not assume that the labor conditions—the wages, hours, and working rules—of the construction industry are without influence in the development of the New York Metropolitan Region. Their influence, as will be pointed out in a later chapter, is felt in numerous ways through the interaction of wage-determining processes in the area, through their effect on the income of the employees of the industry, and through their impact on construction costs in the Region.

We pass from these fairly clear-cut cases of local activities serving consumers in the Region to another group of industries closely tied to its present location—the group which primarily serves other industries rather than the households of the local market. A few such industries have to be in the Region because of overriding transport-cost considerations; tin cans offer a classic illustration.[2] In other cases, the clue to the location of "intermediate" industries in the Region is not transport costs; instead, it lies in the characteristics of the product or service which the industry provides. These characteristics require the industry to maintain its establishments close to their customers. For example, a ship-repair and ship-servicing industry is located in the Port of New York because ships are repaired and serviced at the terminal points of their scheduled runs. Detours or special trips to distant repair facilities would involve significant costs, such as maintaining crews away from home ports.

Quickness of delivery as well as the need for personal contact explain the presence in the Region of other local intermediate industries. These industries principally serve customers who are, as we shall see below, producers of unstandardized products and services and therefore demand products and services tailored to their own requirements. For example, the highly specialized printing industry serves advertising, legal, and financial institutions; the manufacturers producing clasps, buttons, ribbons, belts, and related articles respond quickly to the varying needs of garment manufacturers. Thus the intermediate production requires not only speedy delivery but also immediate and frequent personal contacts with the customers before delivery is made.

Firms catering to the Region's industries, like those catering directly to consumers, are likely to pay labor costs which are higher than those of comparable firms located in many other metropolitan areas of the nation or in smaller communities in the eastern United States. But their concentration on products and services requiring proximity to the customers is likely to offset these higher labor costs. Their location in the Region assures them of the market for their output. In this sense, the intermediate firms may be considered relatively insensitive to labor-cost differences.

It must be borne in mind, however, that the advantages derived from proximity to the market are not as overwhelming for enterprises serving other industries as they are for the activities, such as retailing, which cater to households. Improvements in communication and transportation, such as the development of quick, short-haul trucking service, have been known to shift the locational balance for some intermediate firms or industries toward communities with more attractive labor markets. As already indicated, this has been happening to some extent in the textile dyeing and finishing industry, even though it produces a relatively unstandardized product requiring fairly close contact with the customers. Nevertheless, it is true that, in the present state of the technology and costs of transportation and communication, the vast majority of the firms in the Region's intermediate industries have an overriding need to be near their industrial purchasers.

Communication cost, "external economies," uncertainty

Much of our reasoning about the forces determining the location of local-market industries and services—both those serving the consumer and those serving other industries—applies, of course, to any metropolitan area. Transport cost and proximity to the customers limit the locational choice of retailers, breweries, newspapers, and construction firms in Atlanta as well as in New York. But the New York Metropolitan Region is obviously much more than an administrative and trade center serving a limited hinterland of smaller towns and rural communities. In finance and business management, in business services and in publishing, in entertainment and in manufacturing, the Region's firms "export" services or products to national and even international markets. Can we assume that labor-market considerations play a subsidiary role also in the locational pattern of these industries and services?

The "exporting" industries and services of the Region span such a wide range of economic activity that it is beyond our task to analyze all the forces determining their individual locational patterns. Yet, on the basis of research connected with this and other studies in this series, we conclude that only a very small sector of the industries serving national markets—a sector including about 3 per cent of the Region's employment in the mid-1950's—is primarily oriented in its location toward labor-market conditions. Other factors dominate the locational patterns of most of these industries.

One of these factors is the cost of communication. The need to minimize communication costs constitutes the chief explanation of one of the unique features of the Region's economy—its high concentration of banking and financial institutions, of advertising agencies, of corporate law offices and accounting firms, and of central offices of firms operating in national and broad regional markets. This is one of the major elements making New York the nation's "first city."

The Region's clerical employees in the type of establishments described above are paid higher salaries than similar employees in most—but not all—other metropolitan areas. And they work shorter hours per week than their counterparts anywhere in the nation. But the high cost of New York clerical labor is a minor consideration in the location of these activities. For these offices are also the base for the top executives of the firms involved, executives whose activity calls for personal contacts with suppliers, customers, lawyers, bankers, and accountants, and consequently for a location which facilitates quick and easy communication with all persons outside the firm. The highly unstandardized nature of the communication among all of these activities has led to an agglomeration within a limited geographical area which in the course of time has become a center of financial and other office activities. The advantages of locating in an area facilitating this type of communication are so important that so far they have offset possible differentials in labor costs. But once again a *caveat* about the technology of communication is in order. If once the means could be found for cheap and effective communication between clerks and executives, breaking the tie which requires them to be at a common location, labor costs might well begin to figure in the location of the routine portions of these office activities.

The cost of communication is a significant locational factor in manufacturing, too. Important segments of the garment industries and of such related industries as costume jewelry and handbags are also relatively insensitive to labor-market conditions—a major reason again being the unstandardized nature of their operations and products. But here the situation is a little more complex than in the case of the nonmanufacturing activities.

The products of the garment and related industries are subject to frequent changes in fashion and styling. Moreover, in the higher-priced lines of women's apparel, each product must be held to small quantities. The emphasis on changing product and limited output puts a limit on the size of firms. There are few economies and many risks associated with large-scale operation. The industries consist therefore of hundreds of small producers, each offering a somewhat different product and each attempting to produce a "hit" or to make overnight a copy of a successful design.

Because of the nature of the product and the size of the firms, the communication requirement affects the locational pattern of the firms in two important ways. First, there is the need for face-to-face contact with the army of buyers inspecting the showrooms and fashion shows. Since the firms are small and often cannot maintain their production establishments in separate quarters from their offices and showrooms, the need to locate showrooms in the national shopping center dictates where the other functions will locate. Second, to adjust output to quick changes in style, it is necessary to maintain close contacts with designers and stylists, and to have easy access to the suppliers of highly diverse and unstandardized goods whose color, texture, and pattern have to be fitted into the changing styles and accessories. Location in the Region fulfills these requirements. For some branches of the apparel industry (but not all, as we shall see later), the advantages of proximity to the design center, the suppliers, and the buyers offset such savings in labor costs as might result from location outside the Region.

We are now in a better position to understand why so many specialized intermediate industries are tied to the Region. These industries exist in the Region partly because of the small size of the industrial customers to whom they cater. Firms in such national-market industries as garments, toys, sporting goods, and artificial flowers are generally so small that they are unable to bear the cost of having many needed processes integrated into their own facilities. With not only a highly variable but also a limited output, they cannot afford to take on special-purpose equipment or specialized technicians on a permanent basis. Yet the employment of a more versatile maintenance man or of general-purpose equipment would increase costs. The presence in the Region of the vast array of specialized suppliers, processors, or service units provides the solution for the small firm. The supplier or processor servicing many small firms will, of course, use the specialized type of equipment or labor, and use it at capacity. This makes it possible for the small firm to achieve economies of specialization—"external economies"—by relying on these intermediate industries.

An analogous type of external economy is offered to the Region's small firms by the presence of facilities for small freight shipments. The large number of small shippers makes it possible for freight forwarders to assemble fractional shipments into carloads; indeed, freight forwarding in the Region accounts for 23 per cent of the nation's shipments of this type. In this, as in other services, there are economies associated with the size of the facility. A large firm provides certain services for itself because the size of its output makes it economical to ship by the carload, to have its own power station, or to install its own sewage disposal plant. But to a small firm the economies of size are available only if it locates in a metropolitan area where large numbers of small customers (or taxpayers) warrant an operation of an optimum-size facility by a private firm or a local government. The cost savings derived from the existence of these external economies in the Region reinforce the locational advantage of the communication factor in making the bulk of the small firms in the consumer-goods industries relatively insensitive to potential labor-cost advantages.

And, finally, the economic environment of the Region provides a related, though conceptually different, advantage to the small firms: it facilitates the reduction of uncertainties inevitably involved in planning of inventory and production policies. The clustering of a vast variety of suppliers and service establishments enables the small firms to reduce the amount of funds which have to be committed in inventories, in equipment, or in permanent full-time staffs. This is accomplished by relying on other firms. For example, inventories can be lower than in other locations because unpredicted shortages can be quickly filled from the inventories of many suppliers. Similarly, investment in equipment can be lower than elsewhere because unpredictably large orders can be partly subcontracted to other processors. The amount of capital involved in setting up a new firm can be held at a minimum. In the garment industry and in related consumer industries where the rate of business mortality is very high, this is a critical locational consideration.

In sum, then, the New York Metropolitan Region offers an economic environment which is particularly suitable for business units which specialize in highly unstandardized products or services, and which are barred by size or the nature of the product from achieving economies of large-scale output. For such firms the Region's economy provides a common pool of materials, equipment, and labor. The advantages of relying on this pool are so important for most of the firms in the Region's national-market, small-plant industries with unstandardized products that they overshadow any locational aspects of the Region's labor-market conditions.

Other nonlabor factors

The national-market industries which are found in the New York Metropolitan Region, however, are not simply those whose presence is explained by external economy and communication needs. Some are there for transport reasons. Based in New York, these industries typically ship their goods to markets within a few hundred miles; they are not local industries, therefore, as we use the term, but they are sensitive to the need to minimize their transport costs. Within the market areas they serve, some establishments in this group are tied to the Region by the need of port facilities; sugar refining plants provide an example. Other plants such as those assembling automobiles can choose among locations in the broad radius of a few hundred miles.

Apart from this group, there are others whose presence in the Region seems, on the surface, quite fortuitous or obscure. Sometimes history explains their presence, such as some of the chemical plants whose early financial backers preferred to have them set up close at hand. The presence of others, such as pharmaceuticals, and wire and cables, is less easily explained. If anything holds them in the Region, it seems to be the sunk capital which would have to be scrapped upon leaving their present installations.

Except for the firms which are anchored to the Port, the establishments in these industries would seem to have enough latitude in locating their plants so that they could consciously avoid high wage areas within the broad markets they serve. Most of them, however, belong to a group of industries whose labor policies largely ignore wage differences among geographical locations. Typically the industries to which these plants belong are high wage industries. In some of them, such as chemicals, automobile assembly, and electric cable, many firms have practically uniform wage scales in all their plants, regardless of location. In other industries, such as rubber tires, there are some differences among plants at different locations, but these differences tend to reflect only a small part of the prevailing wage differentials among the areas involved. Even if firms maintain differences in wage levels among their plants for historical reasons, they tend to grant wage increases on a pattern which narrows the regional differentials in percentage terms; flat increases of so many cents per hour, for instance, contribute to such a result. Moreover, "fringe benefits," such as contributions to pension or welfare plans, are frequently uniform from one plant to the next in firms of this sort, even when wage levels are not.

Though there are occasional firms in the group under discussion which constitute exceptions to this general pattern, nevertheless the generalization has considerable validity. The reasons for these policies of wage uniformity, where they exist, have been analyzed elsewhere. It suffices to note here that such firms typically are large concerns with relatively well protected profit margins; that they operate in markets where few competitive manufacturers exist and where a pattern of price leadership prevails; and that they have little to fear in the short run from the possibility of new entrants.[3]

The sluggishness in the response of such firms to opportunities for savings in labor costs stems from still other factors. These firms typically maintain a fairly long planning horizon. That is to say, their policies pertaining to prices, wages, investment, or location reflect considerations of fairly distant future conditions to an extent which is not possible in the case of small enterprises in highly competitive industries. A new location is not likely to be chosen, therefore, if all that it offers is a "short-term" cost advantage over another site.

This outlook is important because savings in wages resulting from location in a low cost area are frequently considered to be of a rather short-run nature. One reason for this is a fairly general belief among managements that interregional wage differences have narrowed in the last two decades and will narrow further in the future. As we shall see in later chapters, there is some factual basis for this view, though not as much perhaps as is popularly supposed. Another reason is that managers of large firms and plants are sometimes prone to regard unionization as inevitable, and they do not generally count on new locations as a means of avoiding collective bargaining. This strengthens their view that interplant wage differences, based on differences in community wage levels, are not likely to be an important economic element in their industries. Again we must emphasize that this is not a universally held view. It appears, however, to be so widely held, at least among large firms, that it constitutes an important factor in locational decisions.

THE LABOR-SENSITIVE ACTIVITIES

We have emphasized more than once that the line dividing the industries which are and those which are not influenced in their location by labor markets is far from hard and fast. The central-office sector and the high priced garment industries are cases in point. We saw earlier that these activities are tied to the New York Metropolitan Region by the advantages of highly developed and specialized "external economies." But it must be understood that the local supply of specialized personnel and skilled labor is an integral part of these external economies. The sheer size of these activities in the Region has fostered specialization among office and garment workers and has attracted to the area labor with particular capabilities in these fields. As a result, a central office or a garment firm obtains the desired type of labor in the Region more easily than in other areas.

To attempt to disentangle cause and effect in the above cases is a fruitless procedure. All we can say is that, though labor-market considerations enter into the locational calculus of these economic units, they are not the dominant element. But, in contrast with these and other economic activities described previously, there are two categories of employment in the Region for which labor-market characteristics are now, and are likely to be in the future, a major factor influencing locational patterns. Though these categories are numerically small at any point in time, they occupy a key position in our analysis.

THE SKILL-ORIENTED SECTOR

One of these categories consists of establishments of considerable size, each of which employs a relatively large number of highly trained workmen or professionals on exacting operations. This category includes establishments producing highly complex special-purpose machinery, specialized electronic equipment, and other instruments and apparatus; such things are commonly built to the specifications of the customers rather than on a mass-production basis. It also includes certain producers of high-style consumer goods, such as very expensive shoes. Then there are various kinds of industrial research facilities which are primarily staffed by highly trained scientists, engineers, and technicians.

The location of such establishments is not affected importantly by considerations of transport cost. The markets which they serve are national in scope, and the transport cost is a small portion of the value of the product; a New York plant, for example, may supply printing presses for newspapers in New Orleans and in San Francisco. Nor are these establishments tied to any special area by the cost of hauling raw materials and supplies. Yet they cannot function successfully unless the area in which they are located contains a large pool of skilled labor.

True, in any given area the "reservoir" of potential labor available to any newcomer is rarely rigidly fixed. For instance, other plants in the area may be raided and workers may be "imported" from other communities or persuaded to commute longer distances than is customary. However, the costs of attracting workers from beyond the immediate commuting distance or of raiding other plants in the locality could easily cancel some of the savings which seem indigenous to the local area.

These considerations have a special significance for manufacturing establishments whose work force consists of many highly skilled workers. For such establishments, locating outside the established industrial centers involves two difficulties: the firm must find a labor market big enough to provide an adequate number of workers with the necessary aptitudes; and the firm must resign itself to a prolonged training period for a major segment of its labor force.

In any location, of course, a manufacturer needing a large number of highly skilled persons is confronted with the problem of training. But a cadre of trained workers is capable of absorbing a limited number of novices without interruption of the work flow. Accordingly, if the manufacturer is in the New York Metropolitan Region or some other large and intensively industrialized metropolitan area, the training of new workers involves a small fraction of the work force at any time. Moreover, because some turnover occurs continually in the other establishments of the area, there is always a possibility of recruiting additional skilled workers from the local labor supply. In contrast, the development of like facilities in a "new" area usually means starting from near-scratch on a lengthy and costly build-up of the labor force.

The prospect of having to build up a large complement of skilled labor and of having to rely on its own training facilities for additional skills constitutes a powerful restraint on the locational choice of a plant with a large skilled complement. Even large urban areas are sometimes not large enough to provide the necessary pool of skills if the areas are not highly industrialized.

For some firms, then, the availability of skilled labor is the key criterion of locational choice. Wage levels are relatively insignificant in their locational decisions. Interregional or intercity differences in wages of skilled workers are considerably smaller than differences in wages of semiskilled or common labor. This is seen in Table 2,

Table 2 Hourly Wages of Selected Skilled and Unskilled Occupations in Manufacturing in Three Metropolitan Areas as Percentage of New York City Wages, 1955–1956

	Skilled	Unskilled
Atlanta	89	74
Memphis	88	71
New Orleans	87	69

Note: Index of skilled occupations derived from wages of skilled maintenance workers in manufacturing plants; index of unskilled occupations derived from wages of workers in the material-moving category. The same occupational weights were used for all areas.

Source: U. S. Bureau of Labor Statistics, *Wages and Related Benefits, 17 Labor Markets, 1955–1956* (Bulletin 1188).

which lists wages of skilled and unskilled occupations in three low-wage metropolitan areas, expressed as a percentage of the corresponding wages in New York City. For instance, though an unskilled worker in Memphis is paid only 71 per cent of an unskilled worker's wage in New York, the ratio for skilled labor comes to about 88 per cent.[4]

Industries employing a large number of highly skilled workers are likely to be insensitive to differences in wage-rate levels for still another reason. In many products requiring craftsmanship, price competition is not very keen—certainly not as keen as competition in more standardized lines. Part of the competitive contest takes the form of emphasis on design and product quality, on speed in working out problems according to specifications, and so on. Whereas the producer of women's shoes retailing at $10 is engaged in a constant struggle to shade his price below that of his competitors, the producer of $30 shoes sells in a market that is relatively insensitive to small price differences. Accordingly, the producer of high-cost shoes is in a position to pay for high-cost labor if such labor is indispensable for style leadership and workmanship. The situation of other employers of high-skill labor, such as producers of specialized custom-built industrial equipment, is analogous.

The problems faced by firms in locating their research facilities are similar to some extent to the considerations discussed above. The ease with which they can recruit the required scientific personnel in a particular area is the major consideration in locational decisions. Because such employees are fairly mobile, there is a national market for scientific services, and interregional salary differentials are not likely to be of any importance. But the mobility of the scientists does not mean that all areas are equally attractive to them. What counts therefore in selecting a location for research facilities is whether scientists and engineers can be either recruited in the area or attracted to it from other communities.

Of course, this does not mean that all research facilities will be located in areas which provide a supply of scientists, engineers, or technicians. Considerations of national security or topographical requirements have placed many laboratories in isolated localities, away from a sizable metropolis. But these are special circumstances. Ordinarily, the ability to recruit scientific personnel is a key determinant to the location of research facilities.

✓ Activities sensitive to labor cost

Earlier we placed considerable stress on the special attractions of the New York Metropolitan Region for various segments of the garment-making complex. But most of these attractions, as we observed, apply primarily to establishments which produce higher priced, more fashionable, less standardized products. The Region also contains firms which specialize in the low-priced lines of the various garment and related industries—industries such as dresses, skirts, men's suits, wallets, shoes, and textile dyeing and finishing.

The balance of forces influencing the location of these firms is quite different from that in the higher-priced lines.

To be sure, the producers at the lower end of the price range also benefit from some of the "clustering" advantages of the Region's economy; but these advantages are not nearly so important for them as for the firms producing at higher prices. The cheaper products are more standardized and are manufactured in large volumes, with relatively long runs for any particular type of dress, shoe, or printed textile materials. Since the ability to be flexible and to change from one style to another is less important in these lines, the advantages of proximity to designers and suppliers are not nearly so significant. Similarly, the work consists largely of relatively routine tasks and can be learned within a short time, and therefore the Region's large supply of highly skilled craftsmen and contractors brings no special locational advantage.

In the lower priced lines of the garment sector, price competition is keen. Survival depends not so much on hitting upon a successful style as on the ability to undersell producers in competing areas. With communication and transport costs relatively small and not varying greatly from one location to another, this ability depends primarily on the size of labor costs per unit of production.

Labor costs are a significant proportion of the total value of product in these low priced lines. Moreover, since the labor is not highly skilled and since the individual establishments are rarely very large, there are many areas which can provide the needed supply of workers. Since labor-market conditions—and particularly levels of wages —vary among these areas, there are labor cost savings which can be achieved by emphasizing labor considerations in the locational choice. What is more, there are numerous locations in which these savings in labor cost are not offset by any increase in other costs.

In the New York Metropolitan Region, the establishments producing low-priced lines of garments and related products constitute the core of the group which is sensitive to labor cost considerations. But the group also includes segments of such industries as electronics, commercial printing, greeting cards, medical supplies, building materials, and textiles. There are portions in each of these industries which operate on a narrow profit margin, produce a relatively standardized product in the lower-priced lines, and sell in a highly competitive market covering broad geographical sections of the country.

The admittedly blurry distinction between establishments that are sensitive to labor costs and those that are insensitive can be illustrated by the situation in the electronics field. Some firms in the Region produce complex electronic apparatus for military and civilian use, and others produce standard component parts such as capacitors or condensers. Skill and precision count heavily in the manufacture of the first group, and price competition is not severe. Accordingly, the level of wages paid to the engineers and production workers is not an important element in locational decisions. But, in the manufacture of standard components, labor cost is a larger share of total cost; mass production for inventory is the rule; the required labor, largely unskilled or semiskilled, performs more or less routine functions. A producer located in a relatively high wage area, therefore, is likely to be under severe competitive pressure from manufacturers with lower labor costs. The analogy to the garment and related trades is very close.

The establishments in the "labor-cost-sensitive" sector, as will become apparent in later chapters, represent the portion of the Region's economy most vulnerable to outside competition. No strong economic factor ties them securely to their present location in the New York area. Since they do not rely heavily on a skilled labor supply, they can find, in many areas, workers whose productivity equals that of their present workers. Indeed, in the case of textile dyeing and finishing, labor productivity outside the New York Metropolitan Region is likely to be higher because of greater willingness on the part of employees to accept increased work-loads. Because the transport costs of these "labor-cost-sensitive" establishments are relatively unimportant, they compete in broad interregional or even national markets with producers from any low wage area. They offer, then, a classical case of interregional competition based to a large extent on the ability to tap sources of cheap labor supply.

THE ACTIVITIES SUMMARIZED

To put the "labor-cost-sensitive" and skill-sensitive industries of the New York Metropolitan Region in solider quantitative perspective, Table 3 presents a breakdown of jobs in the New York Metropolitan Region, by their locational characteristics. Figures of this sort, of course, must not be taken too literally; they involve so many arbitrary decisions of classification and are based upon such imperfect knowledge that they must be thought of as orders of magnitude rather than as precise quantities.

In a crude way, the figures reflect and reaffirm some of the observations of earlier pages. They show the immense importance of local-market activity, much of it in consumer trade and services but

Table 3 Estimated Distribution of Employment in New York Metropolitan Region by Locational Characteristics of Industries [a]

		Percentage of total NYMR employment
Total employment		100.0
Local-market industries		58.8
Consumer trade and services	17.3	
Wholesale, finance, other business services	13.9	
Manufacturing	4.9	
Others	22.7	
National-market industries		41.2
Manufacturing		
Transport-oriented	3.5	
Other manufacturing	19.8	
Wholesale, finance, other business services	7.9	
Others	10.0 [b]	

[a] The breakdown is based partly on 1954 data and partly on 1955 data, and is derived primarily from classifications presented in other volumes in this series.

[b] Included in this figure are a group of self-employed persons whose activities could not be determined; this group accounts for 5.2 per cent of the Region's total employment.

a good deal in other pursuits as well. The local industries, it will be remembered, are largely impervious to wage differences between areas. The figures show, too, that some of the remaining activity in the Region, though catering to wider markets, is principally influenced in its location by transport considerations.

As for that part of national-market manufacturing which is not transport-oriented, comprising 19.8 per cent of the Region's jobs, our classification is so subjective that we have not wished to vest it with the seeming validity which a table of hard numbers seems to impart. But our best guess is that the 19.8 per cent would break down roughly as follows: 2 per cent or a little less in industries whose locational decisions are clearly oriented to various special skill needs; perhaps 10 or 12 per cent in industries whose dominant locational need is external economies of various sorts coupled with the need for speedy and easy communication; perhaps 6 per cent in industries whose locational needs could be satisfied to roughly the same degree almost anywhere in the nation—including many of the mass-production industries like aircraft and some of the chemical groups which tend to pay uniform wages throughout the country; and finally, about 1 per cent or a little more in industries and splinters of industries that are under powerful pressure to find lower labor costs. The latter group, we stress, is made up of bits and pieces of "industries" as any Census classification would define them, differentiated from other plants bearing the same Census title by such subtle characteristics as the degree of style and the price level of their products. Here is where the focus of our interest lies.

2

Skill, Productivity, and Unionization

For those who are principally concerned with the wage position of the New York Metropolitan Region, this chapter is something of a digression. But it is a necessary digression. For when we examine the wage levels of different areas, what we are really after is some rough guide to labor costs; and the two are scarcely the same thing. For one thing, as we observed earlier, the availability of skills is a significant force, not reflected in wage level figures, which can affect the attractiveness of different labor markets; so we shall say here what little more there is to say on that subject. For another, the level of labor costs in any area should depend, at least theoretically, on other considerations besides wages—notably, the productivity of the area's workers, the size and strength of its unions, the nature of the collective bargaining that goes on, and the extent of racketeering. We need to know, therefore, how the New York Metropolitan Region stacks up against other places in these labor-market characteristics and what changes are taking place in the Region's relative position, before we can comfortably proceed with any comparison of wage levels. What we shall conclude is that though these nonwage factors are of some importance in conditioning the wage picture, they do not alter very much the comparative view of labor costs among areas which wages alone afford.

THE POOL OF SKILLS

Not very much is known as yet about trends in the demand for skilled labor in the nation. Nor has it been possible within the limits of the present study to examine that question closely for the New York Metropolitan Region. Yet even without such an examination it is possible to assess the comparative attractiveness of the Region's labor market for employers of skilled personnel.

When compared with most areas of the country, the Region provides a highly favorable environment for such employers. A great majority of skilled workers—probably close to 80 per cent—obtain their skill, know-how, and experience through training on the job.[1] Skills are acquired primarily through upgrading or promotion within a plant and through interplant movement of workers who obtain progressively more complex jobs. In the New York Metropolitan Region there is a large concentration of highly specialized producers in the garment field, in printing machinery and other machinery, in electronic apparatus and scientific instruments. The existence of these firms in the Region provides a training facility with respect to a large variety of skills and perpetuates the area's supply of skilled workers through on-the-job training.[2]

The role of skilled labor in maintaining the economic structure of the New York Metropolitan Region is not confined to providing a satisfactory labor market for the specialized manufacturers who require a large and permanent force of highly trained workers. The area's strength lies also in its ability to meet the highly variable and unpredictable demand for skilled labor on the part of small manufacturers. This is of particular importance to firms specializing in high-quality consumer goods. The normal pattern for many of these firms is one of fairly rapid contraction or expansion of employment, depending on the success of the particular fashion item produced. The strength of the New York area for such firms is that the labor market provides a supply of skilled workers whose primary attachment is to an industry or trade rather than an individual firm, and who shift from one employer to another as some firms expand operations and others contract them. In many other areas, when a slack period forces employers to cut back on their labor force, they often feel obliged to keep their really skilled personnel on the payroll, because of the problems involved in reassembling a skilled force;

but in an area like the New York Metropolitan Region, they have much greater liberty to disperse their skilled workers with every reasonable assurance of reassembling another skilled group on short notice.

And, finally, the New York Metropolitan Region must be considered as one of the more favored locations for research and scientific facilities. Scientists, engineers, and technicians can be recruited relatively easily in the Region. One reason for this is the presence of many institutions of higher learning which provide the recruiting grounds both for advanced scientific personnel and scarce laboratory technicians. A more important reason, perhaps, is the fact that it is easier to attract scientific personnel to a metropolitan laboratory than to one in a less cosmopolitan location. The opportunities for further advanced training at the Region's universities, the possibility of professional contacts with other scientists in the academic world and industry, the cultural amenities offered by New York City—all these factors combine to make the Region an attractive area for scientific and professional workers.

To be sure, the preference among scientific personnel is usually strong for a suburban or "exurban" location, comfortably removed from New York City. But *access* to the City is of paramount importance. As an observer of contemporary industrial life has noted: "An organization's creative and professional people usually will move permanently to a small town only if it is in striking distance of a large city and the professional contacts it affords." [3] The New York area, of course, is not the only metropolitan area in the country which provides such contacts. But it ranks high in these respects. As a result, many industrial research centers in the New York Metropolitan Region are firmly tied to their present location.

At any point in time, therefore, we see an environment very favorable to the location of establishments—both in manufacturing and research—which rely heavily on the services of highly skilled personnel.

It is not possible to give a precise figure representing the Region's employment in the skill-oriented sectors of its economy. On the basis of the 1954 Census of Manufactures and the information collected in the course of our study, a reasonable estimate appears to be that the industries which can be counted in this sector employ about 80,000 to 100,000 people.

This is not a large figure; indeed, it represents only a little over 1.5 per cent of the total employment of the New York Metropolitan Region. But it must be borne in mind that we count here only the industries whose location is *primarily* determined by the pool of skills, and for which other locational considerations are of minor significance. All industries, it is true, use skilled personnel to some extent, and those that depend heavily on the Region's external economies doubtless count the local pool of skills as one of those advantages. But the pool of skills is a critical factor for only a limited number of industries.

We must emphasize, too, that our estimate of the employment of the skill-oriented sector refers to the mid-1950's and that the size and the industrial composition of the sector changes over time with developments of technology and new products.

Though the Region offers notable advantages to skill-oriented producers, the picture is somewhat different when we consider how these advantages may change in the future. There is no doubt that the kind of activities demanding such personnel will continue to expand in the Region. Yet there are good reasons to believe that the Region's advantage as a recruiting ground for skills will shrink.

The development of skills depends most of all on the degree of industrialization in an area. Every large plant, regardless of the general nature of its work force, employs some skilled labor and provides some training opportunities in particular skills. Since the early decades of the present century, we have witnessed a gradual trend toward the equalizing of the degree of industrialization in the various sections of the country. The share of older sections such as New England or the Middle Atlantic states in the nation's industrial employment has been slowly declining; sectional specialization has been decreasing and the country's sections are becoming more uniform in their economic make-up.[4] The industrialization of such areas as the Pacific Coast or the South inevitably means more rapid growth in the local supply of skilled labor.

Another force at work spreading skills to the newer areas is the changing composition of the manufacturing activities in these areas. Although producers of complex equipment must generally locate in a labor market possessing a pool of skilled labor, they also tend to be pulled toward the areas where their main markets exist.[5] As the position of the Northeast in the nation's industrial activity is reduced, other sections are becoming more important as markets for complex machinery or instruments. Hence the rapid economic development of the Pacific Coast is likely to lead to a high rate of expansion of the skill-oriented industries in such metropolitan areas as San Francisco and Los Angeles.

Other factors are working in the same direction. The gradual increase in the education and urbanization of the "newer" sections of the country is facilitating the establishment of research facilities in many areas outside the older cultural and scientific centers. And the same effect follows from improvements in transportation and communication which reduce interregional cultural differences.

Therefore, while the Region does provide a highly favorable environment for the growth of skill-oriented activities, its relative attractiveness in this regard is likely to diminish within the next two or three decades. In the course of the national economic expansion the Region's lead in supply of skilled labor will be reduced as the newer areas acquire the characteristics of the older industrialized and cultural centers.

THE ROLE OF PRODUCTIVITY

Labor cost per unit of output depends not only on the wage level, but also on how much the worker produces for an hour's pay. Wages in an electronic component plant in the borough of Queens may be 10 per cent higher than in a similar plant in North Adams, Massachusetts. But if the productivity of the New York workers were 20 per cent above that of the North Adams work force, the labor costs would be actually lower in Queens. Thus, if there were wide and systematic differences in labor productivity between the New York Metropolitan Region and other areas of the country, a comparison of wage levels would not constitute a useful index of inter-area labor-cost differences.

What can be said about the differences of labor efficiency among various geographical areas and their influence on locational decisions? Measurement of "labor productivity" * from one plant to another involves almost insuperable obstacles. Differences in equipment, in size of plant, in product, or in managerial skills obscure the impact of labor performance on output per man hour. Yet there are a few studies of the problem, studies based mainly on opinions of managements. These studies suggest that manufacturing establishments which employ primarily semiskilled or unskilled labor encounter no important systematic differences in labor efficiency among various geographical locations.[6] The same conclusion emerges from our own interviews and those of colleagues who were charged with investigating certain specific industries. Since these interviews sampled industries which, all told, probably represented a third or more of the manufacturing employment in the Region, we feel reasonably safe in relying upon the conclusion as datum.

It should be noted that these views on the part of management, which are commonly shared by union representatives, appear to be consistent with what we know about the conditions affecting productivity of factory labor. Semiskilled production workers in manufacturing are frequently tenders of highly mechanized equipment. The pace of work and the nature of duties are usually set fairly rigidly by the machine. When the production process is subdivided into many steps, as is done for instance in "section work" on low priced garments, the individual jobs consist of a repetitive operation which can be mastered in a very short time. Highly developed skills or accumulated experience do not enter significantly into this type of work.

To be sure, there are local differences in attitude toward factory

* We have in mind here differences in productivity which can be attributed solely to the variations in the quality of labor.

discipline and in the willingness to work harder to obtain more income, differences which may affect labor efficiency even on routine jobs. There may be differences in absenteeism and turnover rates; in the degree of willingness to take up more responsible assignments; in the response to incentive systems; and in the acceptance of technological changes. If one were to consider two vastly different environments such as, for instance, India and Germany, these intangibles of attitude could be expected to result in wide differences of labor efficiency at any level of skill. But, in such a highly developed and culturally homogeneous country as the United States, sectional differences in the attitude of the labor force toward industrial employment are no longer very significant.[7] Except where major variations exist in plant equipment and layout, in the quality of management, or in the product, the efficiency of labor on routine jobs appears to differ little among the various labor markets of this country. This being true, we incline strongly to the view that relative wage levels and fringe benefits provide a fairly valid index of interregional variations in unit labor costs.

Nevertheless, one should not infer that the question of productivity is disregarded altogether by managements searching for new locations. In practice there is usually some consultation with the local employers and chambers of commerce, an examination of the industrial relations background of the community, and a survey of the type of people registered with the local employment services. But these procedures do not provide a very reliable guide to the productivity of local labor supply.[8] The result is that productivity considerations are reflected only through the crudest sort of indirect impressions. Some firms—not all, by any means—shun the coal-mining regions of the East because of their early history of labor strife; some shun St. Louis because of the dominant position of the Teamsters' Union; and some shun New York City because the local labor is thought to be uncooperative. But no systematic productivity comparisons are attempted.

The point of view that there are no systematic differences in productivity was clearly reflected in the opinions of those New York managers who had acquired personal experience in several geographic locations and thus possessed some basis for comparing the efficiency of the Region's semiskilled or unskilled workers with that of workers in other areas. Insofar as any differences were seen, they were generally attributed to variations in equipment, in products, or in the skills of local management. It is true that preferences were sometimes expressed for location in relatively small communities, generally close to farm areas. In some industries, the view prevailed that workers recruited from a rural environment were more cooperative, harder working, and more "homogeneous" than those in metropolitan areas. On the other hand, in the garment trades the view was commonly expressed that the pace of New York production was faster than that in many small towns. But these views were accompanied by many qualifications and it was generally held that any observable differences in the labor quality among areas were not reliable enough to be of any real importance in locational decisions.

We should also note that insofar as there are still some differences in labor efficiency among particular areas of the country, they are likely to become progressively less important. The very same factors which tend to reduce the Region's initial advantage with respect to the supply of skills—equalization of the degree of industrialization among the country's areas and increase in urbanization—bring about greater homogeneity of the nation's labor forces and create interregional uniformity in attitudes toward industrial employment.[9] Hence, whatever the nonlabor advantages of location in the New York Metropolitan Region, they are not likely to be strengthened in the future by greater efficiency of New York labor. But, by the same token, it follows also that the influx of migrants from outside the Region—whether from Puerto Rico or the rural South—is not likely to lower the efficiency of labor in the area.

COLLECTIVE BARGAINING

Even if the workers of different areas do not display any marked differences in their ability to master relatively simple production tasks, employers might still have considerable preferences for the labor supply of one area as compared with that of another. For, quite apart from any general attitudes toward industrial employment, the labor supply of various areas differs with respect to the extent of unionization and the nature of the local labor organizations.

One possible impact of the local labor organization is obviously in the area of wages and supplementary benefits—a subject discussed in considerable detail in later chapters. But, aside from the issue of wages, there are other aspects of labor organization and collective bargaining which may affect locational decisions. For one thing, collective bargaining sometimes imposes restrictions on work assignments or work-loads and sometimes inhibits the introduction of labor-saving equipment. Moreover, there are other costs involved in collective bargaining, costs which may not be measured in money terms but which are quite real in terms of management's desire to be "boss in its own shop."

Collective bargaining imposes many limitations on management's prerogatives in the plant, limitations relating to layoffs, transfers, promotions, discharges, and other aspects of personnel policy. To some managements these restraints are the most obnoxious aspects of unionism. Managers of small plants who cannot afford professional staffs specializing in various aspects of bargaining are apt to feel particularly strongly about these burdens. And, finally, managers of small establishments are sometimes obliged to think in terms of other burdens which on occasion accompany unionism: extortion, blackmail, involvement with corrupt labor officials. All these factors act as an inducement for management, where it has the choice, to shun labor markets that are strongly unionized.

The New York Metropolitan Region is one of the more strongly unionized areas of the country. Some indication of the strength of unions in the Region is provided in Table 4, which compares the extent of collective bargaining in establishments employing 100 or more workers in large metropolitan areas; in the table, the New York area is represented by New York City and three nearby New

Table 4 Percentage of Employees in Large Establishments[a] Who Are Covered by Collective Bargaining, Selected Areas, 1957–1958

Area[b]	Office workers	Plant workers: All industries	Manu-facturing	Public utilities	Wholesale trade
New York City	10–14	80–84	90–94	95+	70–74
Newark–Jersey City	25–29	85–89	85–89	95+	85–89
Philadelphia	15–19	80–84	85–89	80–84	65–69
San Francisco	15–19	95+	95+	95+	85–89
Los Angeles	20–24	80–84	75–79	95+	75–79
Boston	15–19	70–74	75–79	90–94	50–54
Baltimore	10–14	65–69	80–84	60–64	45–49
Atlanta	15–19	45–49	60–64	70–74	35–39
Chicago	15–19	70–74	70–74	95+	65–69
Milwaukee	25–29	80–84	90–94	95+	n.a.
Minneapolis	10–14	80–84	90–94	95+	85–89
St. Louis	10–14	95–99	95–99	95–99	80–84
New Orleans	5–9	40–44	50–54	95+	5–9

[a] Establishments employing 100 or more workers.

[b] Newark–Jersey City includes Essex, Hudson, and Union Counties; Philadelphia is Philadelphia and Delaware Counties in Pennsylvania and Camden County in New Jersey; Chicago is Cook County. All other areas except New York City are Standard Metropolitan Areas as defined by the Census Bureau.

Source: U. S. Bureau of Labor Statistics, *Occupational Wage Survey* (1957–1958, Bulletin series No. 1224).

Jersey counties. Collective bargaining, it will be seen, is more extensive in this area than in Boston, Philadelphia, Chicago, or Baltimore. As might be expected, it is also more extensive than in any southern metropolitan area. Yet these data probably underestimate the relative strength of unionism in the Region. In the nation as a whole, the extent of organization is generally greater in large plants than in smaller ones.[10] But the Region's garment industries and related industries—all composed mainly of small plants—are almost completely unionized. Accordingly, if Table 4 were complete in its coverage, the Region's preeminent position as a unionized area would stand out even further.

Besides, the comparison in Table 4 is with some of the most

strongly organized areas in the United States. No comparable figures are available for the country as a whole. But relatively rough calculations give us an estimate of 68 per cent as the proportion of United States manufacturing workers covered by collective bargaining.[11] Beyond doubt this figure is considerably lower than the equivalent proportion for the Region, which probably runs on the order of 80 to 85 per cent.

But, though unionism is strong in the New York Metropolitan Region, collective bargaining in the area is not a monolithic force impressing uniform systems of labor-management relations upon employers. On the contrary, collective bargaining in the Region is characterized by a wide diversity of forms and policies, corresponding to the wide range of the local industries and services.

The large industrial plants of the mass-production industries—automobiles, aircraft, tin cans, rubber products, chemicals, electric cable, and others—represent one type of collective bargaining. Here the bargaining is generally with locals belonging to the national industrial unions, such as the United Rubber Workers or the International Union of Electrical Workers. The nature of collective bargaining is essentially the same whether the plant is in Newark, Cleveland, or South Bend. There are, of course, many differences among particular establishments. But in broad outline the policies of the local unions, each consisting entirely of workers in a particular establishment, reflect industrywide or national wage patterns adjusted slightly to local conditions.

In plants of this sort, the similarity between the Region and other industrialized areas extends to all aspects of labor-management relations, not only wages but also limitations on work-loads and restraints on labor-saving devices. Unions in the mass-production industries do not generally attempt to restrict productivity,[12] and New York unions do not differ from those elsewhere in this respect. This, at least, is the conclusion to which our field work clearly points.

Of course, the managements of these plants are burdened with contractual provisions pertaining to many aspects of the operations.

But the limitations are not locationally important, because they exist in very much the same form in different localities. The industries of these plants are strongly unionized throughout the country. Nor could local corruption among union officials, if it existed, make itself heavily felt in dealings with these large plants. The power and scale of corporations in this category renders them largely impervious to any major extortions in a local market.

The pattern of collective bargaining in the garment industry complex, in services, and in construction is quite different. Here the firms are typically small while the local union, consisting of employees of many firms, is relatively large. When a large local union bargains with a small firm, the union could become the sole administrator of the contract. Yet this is not the typical situation in the New York Metropolitan Region. The problems of small firms facing a large local have been reduced somewhat by the institution of multi-employer bargaining and by the functioning of employers' associations.[13]

Bargaining through employer groups takes many forms in the Region. The powers assigned to the employer associations by individual firms and the geographical coverage of the agreement vary from one industry to another. But in many cases the employer association not only negotiates labor contracts for its members but also plays a role in the subsequent settlement of union grievances and other problems arising during the lifetime of the contract. Moreover, the existence of employers' associations facilitates the creation of arbitration machinery for the local industry. The total result is that the small firm achieves a stronger bargaining position and obtains many advantages which ordinarily could not be obtained without employing industrial relations experts.[14]

The presence of multi-employer bargaining does not free individual employers from the rules of "industrial jurisprudence" which are imposed by collective bargaining. And some of the rules imposed by unions undoubtedly have adverse effects on labor efficiency. But such rules appear to be of importance primarily in construction, an industry strongly tied to its present location by market considerations.[15] Hardly any restrictions on productivity exist in the large complex of industries making garments and other light consumer goods. An outstanding exception is the textile dyeing and finishing industry, in which the negotiated work-loads are lower in the New York Metropolitan Region than elsewhere. We shall discuss some of the factors underlying the differences in the negotiated work-loads in a later chapter.

Multi-employer bargaining is much more prevalent in the New York Metropolitan Region than in the country as a whole.[16] But the Region also contains many industries in which employer groups do not cover all the firms. In some cases, the bargain negotiated by the association is almost automatically extended to such firms without major modifications. In other cases, the establishment involved may enter into a separate bargain with a union local composed entirely of its own employees; in that case, the contract signed is likely to reflect the special conditions of the firm. It is impossible to draw universally valid conclusions pertaining to such numerous individual contracts negotiated in the Region; our interviews do suggest, however, that the smaller firms in industries such as paperboard boxes, paint, and photographic supplies, operating under individual contracts, do not find the contract provisions particularly oppressive. More explicitly, the union-imposed rules are not considered as a major deterrent to location in the New York Metropolitan Region.

Everything we have said suggests that collective bargaining in the New York Metropolitan Region, though inevitably imposing some limitations on managerial discretion, is not generally more restrictive than in other *unionized* areas. Firms which expect to deal with unions would not find great differences between union policies in the Region and those elsewhere. In addition, the Region is not, on the whole, an area of especially sharp labor-management conflict—not, at any rate, in most of the industries which have locational choice. Nevertheless, it is obvious that establishments which are determined to avoid unionization *per se* must consider the Region's labor market as an unacceptable prospect in their locational considerations.

What kind of firms would fall into this latter category? Judging from the results of our field work, unionization of the Region's market is a locational deterrent principally in the case of small and medium-sized firms which want to locate somewhere in the Northeast but which are not restricted to any particular location by transport costs, requirements of high labor skill, or other factors. In such cases the impact of unionization usually operates as an influence which is additive to other factors, notably wages and rent. Being free to locate within a fairly wide geographic area, such firms can obtain sites in smaller communities where such costs are lower than in the New York Metropolitan Region. Hence their avoidance of the Region is generally motivated by a number of considerations, of which unionization is one and probably only in rare cases the most important one.

What of the future? Since the end of World War II, the union movement in the United States has grown at a rate roughly equal to that of the nonagricultural labor force. There are some persuasive reasons for believing that the proportion of the nonagricultural labor force organized by unions—now about 35 per cent—will not increase in the next twenty years.[17] Nevertheless, the rate of union growth will differ among geographical areas; unions will undoubtedly grow faster in the less extensively organized areas which experience a higher rate of industrialization than in the older industrialized sections of the country.[18] One may thus expect that the locational significance of unionization, which in our view is already rather limited, will be still further reduced in future decades as the geographical distribution of collective bargaining becomes more uniform throughout the country.

RACKETEERING

There is still another aspect of unionism which merits a brief discussion—labor racketeering and extortion. Our interest lies, of course, in its locational significance.

Labor racketeering tends to develop in industries and services in which individual firms are small in relation to the union and in which even a short strike can expose the employer to severe losses.

These conditions are generally found in services, the construction trades, and the delivery of highly perishable products like fruits and vegetables. In very large metropolitan areas, including the New York Metropolitan Region, a great many enterprises fit this description. Hence there are considerable opportunities for corrupt union officials to sell "strike insurance" and considerable incentive for employers to buy it.

The existence of corruption in labor-management relations therefore depends much more on the conditions of the industry than it depends on the area of the country where the industry is located. The corruption which has cropped up from time to time in the garment trades, in trucking, and in the wholesaling of perishable foods will tend to occur wherever these activities have developed on a large scale, so long as the industry consists of small firms easily exposed to bankruptcy.

The incidence of corruption in the various services or industries of the Region has rarely had locational implications. Typically, racketeering and extortion have taken place in industries tied to their location by the need of proximity to their markets—that is, in local trucking, construction, and consumer services. One exception, however, is the garment industry—and specifically the highly competitive section of the women's dress industry producing inexpensive dresses.

Racketeering gained a foothold in this industry as a result of the jobbers' efforts to find contractor shops which would undercut union pay scales. Such contractor shops were generally found only outside the strongly unionized area of Manhattan. Strong-arm men were retained to move the goods by truck between the cutting rooms of the jobbers and the nonunion shops where the cheap dresses were sewed, and then back to the showrooms in Manhattan. Eventually, however, this "service" was forced upon some firms, whether or not they wanted it. Finally, the racketeering elements, though originally established in the trucking operations, appear to have branched out into the contracting business in some areas of Pennsylvania. In the end, therefore, the racketeers not only provided the transportation but also designated the contracting shops to which their jobber clients were to send out cloth for sewing.[19]

The existence of racketeering in the dress industry has been a problem for the International Ladies' Garment Workers' Union. Yet we should not attach too much locational significance to this phenomenon. The movement of contracting shops to locations outside of the Region would have taken place in any case, reflecting the relative wage position of the area and the intense price competition in the industry. But the existence of some racketeer-dominated shops in the smaller communities outside of the Region provides another illustration of the fact that it is the economic structure of the particular industry rather than its geographic location which largely determines the ability of the racketeer to enter the labor-management relations scene.

THE WAGE-ORIENTED SECTOR

Of all the nonwage characteristics of the labor market that we have discussed, the only one that appears to be of real importance is the supply of skills. Our discussion has minimized the locational significance of inter-area differences in labor productivity and unionization. To minimize those aspects is to emphasize the importance of the other determinants of labor costs—wages and fringe benefits. In industries in which labor cost differences loom as an important determinant of location, the attractiveness of the Region will be primarily determined by the local wages and benefits as compared with those in other areas. In this sense the activities which fall in the labor-cost-sensitive sector may be termed "wage-oriented" in their locational pattern, and we shall refer to them by this name from now on.

As of the mid-1950's, it appears that the establishments in the wage-oriented sector of the New York Metropolitan Region had about 60,000 to 80,000 employees. As already indicated, most of these were in the low-priced lines of garment-making and related manufacturing; others were in selected lines of electronics, printing, and a few additional industries.

Though this is a tiny figure compared with the Region's massive total of about seven million jobs, the reader will recognize by now that this figure is not to be taken as a full measure of the influence of labor-market conditions on the Region's development. The composition of the wage-oriented sector is not fixed for all time; on the contrary, the sector is a revolving group. Even if the jobs now in this sector pass from the local scene, the New York Metropolitan Region is still bound to have a slice of employment acutely sensitive to wage differentials among geographical areas.

The very fact that the wage-oriented sector is continually replenished by the changing nature of industry necessitates our considering in detail the economic position of the sector as presently constituted. We must examine the wage environment in which the sector exists—the trends in its wage standing as compared with its competitors in other areas and the changes in its relative position in the Region's economy. Through such an examination we can gain an insight into the economic forces by which the labor market exerts influence on whatever constitutes the wage-oriented sector of the Region at any point of time—including the future—and hence can perceive the labor-market impact on the location of economic activity in the New York Metropolitan Region.

3

Wages and Fringe Benefits

It would shorten our story considerably if we could leap from the discussion which went before to an analysis of the wage situation in the 60,000 or 80,000 jobs in the Region which we have called wage-oriented. But any such short-cut would be exceedingly dangerous. To gain an adequate picture of the role which wage levels may play in the Region's development, we are obliged to consider the levels of wages and fringe benefits in a broad range of the Region's industries and services.

One reason why the whole wage position of the Region merits scrutiny has already been made clear. Economic activities—whether whole industries or specialized product lines—change over time; some which now are not wage-oriented will enter that category in the future.

Another reason for studying wages in the Region generally—not merely in wage-oriented firms—is that the wage structure of the Region is the product of interaction among a variety of industries. One cannot effectively assess the pressures on wage-oriented activities unless he can picture those activities in relation to the Region's total wage structure. It is particularly difficult for a firm under wage pressure to remain in a particular area if the *general* wage level of the area continues to exceed the wage levels of other labor markets. For such a firm is apt to find itself squeezed between external pressure on its ability to sell its products and local pressure on its ability to obtain an adequate labor supply.*

Finally, our curiosity about the general wage position of the Region derives from our interest in furnishing data that might throw

* The significance of this problem is discussed in Chapter 5.

light on the Region's future growth. Economic activities—not merely wage-oriented ones—are continually shifting among geographical areas, for many complex reasons. Some activities will expand in the New York Region faster than others. They may be drawn toward the Region for reasons that have little or nothing to do with labor; yet, at the same time, wages may exert some influence on the rate of the expansion. If our wage comparisons were confined to the industries represented in the wage-oriented sector, those who wish to project the industrial make-up of the Region would receive no clue about how comparative wage levels might affect other industries.

One last point, before proceeding with the analysis. How reliable are the data presented in the following pages? Appendix A deals with the question from the technician's point of view. Here we need say only that there are many limitations inherent both in the problem of interregional wage comparisons and in the data themselves, but that the statistical material analyzed here presents a fairly accurate broad picture of the wage position of the New York Metropolitan Region. This does not mean, of course, that the wage comparisons between the Region and other areas reflect exactly the respective wage differences for each particular industry analyzed here. As is pointed out in the appendix, there are numerous reasons why any available wage data could not provide an exact picture of interregional wage variations. One must not accept each figure literally as an unerring measure of wage levels or other labor-cost levels. Furthermore, we were not always able to make adequate estimates for the entire 22-county Region, and therefore in some of our tables the Region is represented by a smaller geographical area. Nevertheless, when all this has been said, we may still consider our statistical material as a fairly reliable guide to the wage structure in the New York Metropolitan Region and its relation to such structures in other labor markets.*

* Throughout this study we shall deal with averages of wage payments in different locations. It should be recognized, however, that in any area there is always a dispersion of wages for the same occupation employed in different firms. Accordingly, even though Area A has a higher *average* than Area B, there are likely to be some firms in Area B that pay higher wages than some firms in Area A.

AVERAGE EARNINGS COMPARED

If we begin by examining one of the simplest measures of wages, our first impression is that wages in the Region are not particularly high relative to those of several other areas. Table 5 shows the aver-

Table 5 Average Weekly Earnings in Selected Metropolitan Areas, Selected Occupations in All Employment Categories, Winter 1955–1956

(metropolitan areas as percentages of New York–Newark–Jersey City area)

New York–Newark–Jersey City area	100.0
Detroit	106.6
San Francisco	106.5
Chicago	104.1
Los Angeles	104.0
Portland	100.2
Milwaukee	97.4
St. Louis	96.0
Minneapolis–St. Paul	92.9
Philadelphia	91.4
Denver	90.9
Atlanta	85.3
Dallas	83.7
Providence	83.4
Memphis	80.1
New Orleans	76.4

Notes: The New York–Newark–Jersey City area includes the five boroughs of New York City and the New Jersey counties of Essex, Hudson, and Union. Chicago is Cook County only; Philadelphia is Delaware and Philadelphia Counties in Pennsylvania and Camden County in New Jersey. All other areas are Standard Metropolitan Areas as defined by the Census Bureau.

In computing the earnings we used the occupational composition of the New York–Newark–Jersey City area. The number of occupations which we used varied from 57 to 61, depending on the area with which the New York–Newark–Jersey City area was compared. All workers were assumed to work a 40-hour week. In most areas, including the New York–Newark–Jersey City area, the establishments are those of over 100 employees.

Source: U. S. Bureau of Labor Statistics, *Occupational Wage Survey* (Bulletin series No. 1188).

age weekly earnings of a large group of occupations in plants and offices of fifteen other metropolitan areas, expressed as a percentage of the Region's earnings in the same occupations. The Region is represented here by New York City and three industrial counties of New Jersey—a combined area which has about three-fourths of the Region's employment. The New York area, according to the table, ranks below the two largest metropolitan areas in the Midwest and below the three Pacific Coast areas that are listed. On the other hand, the New York area ranks high in relation to other centers in the East and the South.

This result may appear surprising to New York businessmen hard pressed by what they consider "high local wages." But one must not forget a critical point in interpreting the data in Table 5. The statistics on average earnings in various occupations reflect not only the different levels of wages paid in various metropolitan areas but also the differences in the industrial composition of those areas. The industrial composition—or "mix"—of an area affects its average wage; workers in steel mills or oil refineries are paid more than those in garment shops, and, when steelworkers dominate in an area instead of garment workers, this fact alone is bound to raise the average wage of the area.

Yet in some respects Table 5 overstates rather than understates the average level of wages in the Region. Because no manufacturing establishment with less than 100 workers is included in the Region's data, the wages of a very large number of firms in the garment industries and related activities are not reflected in the comparison. And these industries pay low wages compared with manufacturing as a whole.

Table 6, however, partially meets this last problem. In this table, which pertains to manufacturing only, the average hourly earnings for all the manufacturing firms in the 17-county Standard Metropolitan Area * are compared with those in a number of major cities

* The Census Bureau calls this the "New York–Northeastern New Jersey Standard Metropolitan Area." In this book we will ordinarily shorten it to "New York Standard Metropolitan Area," or, in appropriate cases, simply to

Table 6 Average Hourly Earnings in Manufacturing, Selected Cities, 1955

(cities as percentage of New York Standard Metropolitan Area)

New York Standard Metropolitan Area	100.0
New York City	98.4
Newark–Jersey City	102.6
Detroit	121.9
San Francisco	114.6
Milwaukee	110.4
Portland	109.9
Los Angeles	108.8
Chicago	108.3
Minneapolis	102.6
St. Louis	101.6
Philadelphia	101.0
Denver	99.5
Boston	93.2
New Orleans	89.1
Atlanta	87.5
Memphis	84.4
Providence	82.5
National average	97.9

Source: U. S. Bureau of Labor Statistics, *Employment and Earnings* (June 1957).

and with the national average. These figures reflect the influence of the "industry mix" on the average earnings of the New York area, and they show, too, the significance of the low-wage sector. Ten of the cities, strung across the country from Philadelphia to San Francisco, have higher average hourly earnings in manufacturing than the New York area.

Though the figures so far presented cannot answer the questions of the producer in a specific industry who is seeking an area where

the "Standard Metropolitan Area," as above. The five counties which are in the New York Metropolitan Region but not in the Standard Metropolitan Area are Orange, Dutchess, and Putnam in New York State; Monmouth in New Jersey; and Fairfield in Connecticut.

labor costs are low for his industry, they do have a significance for our study. By indicating the general levels of community wages, they suggest that certain types of industries would not find it too difficult to attract workers in the New York Metropolitan Region. A television set assembly plant, for instance, paying its production workers about $1.80 per hour, might find it difficult to attract a qualified complement of workers in Detroit, where employment is heavily weighted by the high-wage automobile industry. But in the New York Region this wage would compare favorably with wages in many other local industries. The plant might thus encounter no problem in attracting workers from these alternative sources of employment. In this sense, the average manufacturing wage in the community does have some bearing on industrial location of particular enterprises. It is apparent from the data in Tables 5 and 6, therefore, that many relatively high-wage industries would not encounter difficulties in "keeping up" with the New York Metropolitan Region in terms of wages, and would not find that the Region's community wage structure was a bar to location.

On the basis of these figures, however, we cannot go much further. For a more precise picture of the wage position of the New York Metropolitan Region, we must turn to a consideration of wages in individual industries. The first industries to be discussed are those containing wage-oriented activities.

INDUSTRIES UNDER WAGE PRESSURE

Garment and related industries

As we have seen, there are some activities in the New York Metropolitan Region which are under pressure to find a location in which labor costs are at a minimum. Typical of such activities are various segments of the intricate complex represented by the garment industries and related industries—a complex employing about 400,000 workers in the New York Metropolitan Region. The 400,000 jobs vary in the degree of their sensitivity to the wage factor. Most of them are linked to a New York location without regard to labor

Table 7 Average Hourly Wages in Nine Garment and Related Industries, 1955

(selected areas as percentage of New York Metropolitan Region)

	Men's suits and coats	Women's, misses' coats and suits [a]	Women's underwear and nightwear	Corsets and allied garments	Knit outerwear	Footwear	Millinery	Men's, boys' dress shirts [b]	Finishing and dyeing of textiles (synthetic) [c]
East									
NYMR	100.0	100.0	100.0	100.0	100.0	100.0	100.0	100.0	100.0
Boston	89.1	87.1	83.7	n.a.	94.5	81.4	64.4	n.a.	n.a.
New England	n.a.	n.a.	n.a.	n.a.	n.a.	n.a.	n.a.	n.a.	91.4
Philadelphia	90.1	94.0	82.3	n.a.	89.0	88.3	90.1	n.a.	n.a.
Pottsville-Shamokin, Pa.	n.a.	n.a.	n.a.	n.a.	n.a.	n.a.	n.a.	86.9	n.a.
Baltimore	n.a.	86.6	n.a.	n.a.	n.a.	n.a.	n.a.	82.4	n.a.
Maryland Eastern Shore	n.a.	n.a.	n.a.	n.a.	n.a.	n.a.	n.a.	80.7	n.a.
Southeastern U. S.	n.a.	n.a.	n.a.	n.a.	n.a.	n.a.	n.a.	n.a.	73.1
Midwest									
Cleveland	n.a.	n.a.	n.a.	n.a.	84.1	n.a.	n.a.	n.a.	n.a.
Chicago	85.4	102.8	105.0	93.5	89.0	n.a.	n.a.	n.a.	n.a.
St. Louis	81.3	n.a.	86.5	n.a.	n.a.	81.4	69.1	n.a.	n.a.
Milwaukee	n.a.	n.a.	n.a.	n.a.	n.a.	81.9	n.a.	n.a.	n.a.
Cincinnati	92.2	n.a.	n.a.	n.a.	n.a.	76.1	n.a.	n.a.	n.a.
Kansas City	n.a.	76.9	n.a.	n.a.	n.a.	n.a.	n.a.	n.a.	n.a.
Far West									
Los Angeles	97.4	98.4	87.9	87.6	82.8	87.2	81.7	98.7	n.a.
San Francisco	n.a.	86.9	n.a.	n.a.	n.a.	n.a.	n.a.	n.a.	n.a.

Notes and sources on page opposite.

costs. But others—notably jobs in low-priced lines in their respective industries—are under unrelenting pressure to find the areas where labor costs are lowest.

Table 7 presents a comparison between the New York Metropolitan Region and certain other metropolitan areas in respect to average hourly wages in nine garment and related industries for 1955. The wages in the other areas are expressed as a percentage of corresponding wages in the New York Metropolitan Region. The picture emerging, though not completely reliable in all details, is clear enough. In comparison with other centers of manufacturing the Region is a high wage area in almost every industry listed in the table. An exception to the pattern is Chicago's wages in two of the in-

---

NOTES AND SOURCES FOR TABLE 7

n.a. = not available.

Note: The technical details of the method used in constructing this table are indicated below and further discussed in Appendix A. Except in three industries, as noted below, the percentages were computed from average hourly earnings in 1955, names of cities stand for Standard Metropolitan Areas, and NYMR means the 22 counties of the New York Metropolitan Region.

[a] Computed from occupational earnings of selected occupations. The occupational composition of the New York Metropolitan Region, as represented in this industry by ten counties in the New York–Newark–Jersey City–Paterson area, was used as weights. Chicago area is represented by Cook County only; Philadelphia area comprises Delaware and Philadelphia Counties in Pennsylvania and Camden County in New Jersey. The comparison is for 1957. Though women's skirts are a part of the same Census industry as coats and suits, skirts are *not* included in the present comparison.

[b] Computed from occupational earnings of selected occupations. The occupational composition of the New York Metropolitan Region, as represented by seven counties of the New York–Elizabeth–Newark area, was used in weighting. The comparison is for 1956.

[c] Computed from occupational earnings of selected occupations. The occupational composition of the New York Metropolitan Region, as represented by Bergen and Passaic Counties, was used in weighting. To ensure greater comparability, the wage data used refer only to the branch of the industry processing synthetic broad woven fabrics (including silk). This branch represents the bulk of employment in textile dyeing and finishing in the Region. The comparison is for 1956.

Sources: Special tabulations of the U. S. Bureau of Labor Statistics and the New York State Department of Labor; BLS, *Women's and Misses' Coats and Suits, 1957,* Forms OWR–24 for individual areas; BLS, *Men's and Boys' Dress Shirts and Nightwear, 1956,* Forms OWR–24 for individual areas; BLS, *Textile Dyeing and Finishing* (BLS Report No. 110).

dustries.[1] But, generally speaking, New York's wages appear to be significantly higher than those of other areas, usually by as much as 10 per cent.

Since the bulk of the jobs in the wage-oriented sector are in the garment industry complex, these data are highly suggestive of the competitive position of the Region's producers. To be sure, wages are not equally important as a locational factor in all of the industries listed in Table 7. For example, wages are a smaller proportion of the total value of the product in "corsets and allied garments" than in the outerwear industries. And in an industry like men's suits and coats the wage data probably overstate the competitive disadvantage of the Region's manufacturers because some of the other areas may not have so large a proportion of high-skill workers as does New York.[2] But, in our view, Table 7 accurately conveys the essential idea that in these industries wages are significantly higher in the Region than in the other major centers of production.[3]

Table 8 presents a wage comparison between the New York Metropolitan Region and other centers of manufacturing in the largest industry in the garment sector—women's and misses' dresses. The wage position of the Region in this major industry is very much the same as in the other industries in the garment complex. The Region pays considerably higher wages than the other manufacturing centers.

But the competitive handicap imposed by New York's wage levels in the garment and related industries is even greater than appears in Tables 7 and 8. For, in some cases, the critical competition for New York producers comes from smaller communities and rural districts rather than from other large metropolitan areas. Unfortunately, it is difficult to obtain wage data for these smaller communities, except through costly special surveys. What these data would show, however, is suggested by the figure for Wilkes-Barre and Hazleton in Table 8 for the women's and misses' dress industry. Except for Dallas, this area has the lowest wage reported in the table, more than 40 per cent below that of the New York area.[4] Yet even the Dallas area—low though its wages are—appears to be un-

Table 8 Average Hourly Wages in Women's and Misses' Dress Industry, 1955

(selected manufacturing centers as percentage of New York area)

East	
New York area	100.0
Boston	82.2
Philadelphia	89.5
Wilkes-Barre and Hazleton, Pa.	58.9
Midwest	
Cleveland	75.8
Chicago	86.4
St. Louis	72.2
South	
Dallas	58.9
Far West	
Los Angeles	85.4

Notes: This is the industry sometimes known as "Dresses, unit-priced." Average wages were computed from selected occupational earnings. The occupational composition of the New York area was used as weights for individual occupations. The New York area means ten counties, including New York, Newark, Jersey City, and Paterson and their surroundings; these ten counties contain nearly all of the New York Metropolitan Region's plants in this industry. All other areas except Chicago and Philadelphia are Standard Metropolitan Areas. Chicago is represented by Cook County only; Philadelphia means Delaware and Philadelphia Counties in Pennsylvania and Camden County in New Jersey.

Source: U. S. Bureau of Labor Statistics, *Women's and Misses' Dresses, 1955,* Forms OWR-24 for individual areas.

der wage pressure from its own rural competitors. It is reported that some dress manufacturing firms in Dallas have found it difficult to survive there because of competition in low labor cost from rural communities of northern Texas.[5]

Accordingly, we must bear in mind the existence of the rural communities when we think of the competitive position of the New York Metropolitan Region.[6] True, the goods manufactured in those communities may be of relatively cheap type and not comparable with the bulk of the Region's production; nevertheless, the output in those communities still imposes severe competitive pressure on the Region's firms which produce cheaper lines. Indeed, in such industries as women's dresses, men's shirts, or footwear, it is the competition of producers in places other than large metropolitan areas that provides most of the pressure exerted on the New York Metropolitan Region.[7]

The wage data presented in Tables 7 and 8, of course, compare the various areas without regard to the price lines of goods produced in a particular location. Since we are aware that the lower-priced lines are under the greatest pressures to reduce labor costs, these lines merit particular attention. For the most important of the industries, women's and misses' dresses, it is possible to gain some indication of the wage competition which faces New York's lower-price producers. From a study conducted by the Bureau of Labor Statistics in 1955, it is apparent that in New York City the largest groups of workers making dresses selling for less than $6.75 wholesale are (1) female sewing machine operators working on a so-called "tailor system," and (2) men cutters.[8] In Table 9, the wages of these two occupations in the low-priced line in New York are compared with the wages of the corresponding occupations in other areas. Because no division of wages by price lines was available for the other areas, all price lines are included for them. The table shows that the wages of the workers producing the cheaper products in New York are higher than the wages of workers employed in all price groups in other areas; only Philadelphia deviated from the pattern.

The implication of the data in Table 9 is apparent. The practice in the women's dress industry is to vary the wages for a given skill according to the price line.[9] Therefore the wages outside New York in the less-than-$6.75 price line must be significantly lower than those shown in the table—probably as much as 10 or 15 percentage points lower.[10]

The comparison in Table 9 does not include wages in the Wilkes-Barre and Hazleton area. The reason is that the dress industry in

Table 9 Average Hourly Wages of Two Prinicpal Dress Occupations, Lowest Price Line in New York City Compared with All Price Lines Elsewhere, 1955

(selected areas as percentage of New York City)

	Female sewing machine operators, tailor system	Male cutters
East		
New York City	100.0	100.0
Boston	95.6	87.5
Philadelphia	111.0	92.4
Midwest		
Cleveland	n.a.	77.4
Chicago	98.3	94.4
St. Louis	82.3	71.2
South		
Dallas	66.3	60.4
Far West		
Los Angeles	93.4	92.7

n.a. = not available.

Note: The data for New York represent only that portion of the women's and misses' dress industry which makes dresses selling for less than $6.75 wholesale. All areas except New York City, Chicago, and Philadelphia are Standard Metropolitan Areas. Chicago and Philadelphia are represented by the same areas as in Table 8.

Source: See Table 8 source.

that area uses the section system and does not have tailor-system operators. But a comparison analogous to that in Table 9 can be made if we compare average hourly wages in Wilkes-Barre and Hazleton with those in New York City contract shops which produce dresses selling at less than $6.75 wholesale. Such a comparison reveals that the wages in these Pennsylvania cities are 32.7 per cent below those of New York.[11] Thus again it becomes apparent that the low-price producers of New York pay significantly higher wages than their competitors outside.

Fringe benefits in apparel industries

The picture of the pressures on New York producers in the garment industries would be incomplete without some exploration of the part played by supplementary employee remuneration, that is, by "fringe benefits"—unemployment compensation, workmen's compensation, paid vacations and holidays, pension plans, medical and hospitalization insurance, and the like. The importance of considering this complex and elusive aspect of labor cost, indeed, is all the greater because of numerous indications that it is growing even more rapidly than the direct wage bill.

For example, a survey by the U. S. Department of Commerce—covering fringe benefits required by law and expenditures on private pension and welfare plans, and excluding many items such as paid vacations, holidays, and shift premiums—indicated that between 1940 and 1955, fringe payments rose from 4.6 per cent of wages and salaries to 6.1 per cent.[12] The Chamber of Commerce of the United States, surveying 124 large industrial companies in 1947 and 1955, indicated that their fringe payments *of all kinds*—including vacations, paid holidays, and also such items as paid lunch periods and bonuses—rose in this period from 15.1 to 21.7 per cent of wages and salaries.[13]

Though our knowledge concerning the exact amounts of money involved in the various types of employee benefits is very limited, and though even the concepts of such benefits have not yet been sharply defined,[14] it is still possible to gain a fairly good impression of the relative position of the New York Metropolitan Region in some of the apparel industries. The available data show that the fringe benefits generally tend to accentuate the wage differences in these industries between New York and the lower wage areas.

Let us first consider the two largest industries in the women's garment group—(1) women's and misses' dresses and (2) women's and misses' coats and suits.[15] Aside from such legally required payments as unemployment insurance taxes and old-age insurance taxes, the most important expenditures on fringe benefits in these industries are the payments that employers make for health and welfare benefits, vacations, and retirement. These payments have been agreed upon in the process of collective bargaining with the International Ladies' Garment Workers' Union. In most metropolitan areas, the benefits are fully financed by the employers, who contribute a sum, fixed as a given percentage of the payroll, to a local fund jointly administered by the union and employers. Where the employer provides vacation pay directly to the worker—as he does in some areas—it is easy to translate this pay into percentage-of-payroll terms for comparisons between areas.

Table 10 shows the pattern of employer contributions to health and welfare benefits, vacations, and retirement in the major production centers of the two basic women's garment industries as developed through collective bargaining agreements.* In its fundamentals, the picture presented in the table is quite clear. Almost without exception, the New York Metropolitan Region, as represented by ten counties, provides higher benefits than other labor markets, enhancing the labor-cost disadvantages of the New York producers.

But the data in Table 10 do not tell the whole story. Not all the labor markets are unionized to the same extent, and in some the union is relatively weak. For instance, in women's dresses Dallas appears to be a center where nonunion shops are of particular importance; Los Angeles, too, seems to have a relatively large group of nonunion plants. Though the coat-and-suit industry is probably more uniformly organized, Los Angeles seems to have several nonunion shops. Surveys by the Bureau of Labor Statistics indicate that in these and other areas the benefits in nonunion shops are generally very limited, particularly with respect to employer-financed retirement plan and health benefits. Thus, the higher cost of supplementary employee remuneration in the New York area is due not only to the fact that union-negotiated benefit contributions are generally higher than union-negotiated contributions in other areas, but also

* The figures are based on 1955 and 1957 contributions, but the picture has not changed materially since. One change has been an equalization between New York and Philadelphia in the dress industry.

Table 10 Fringe Benefits in Two Women's Garment Industries in Principal Production Centers[a]

(estimated employer contributions expressed as a percentage of wages paid)

	Women's and misses' dresses, 1955	Women's coats and suits, 1957
	East	
New York area	8.5[b]	9
Boston	6.5	6.5
Philadelphia	9	7
Wilkes-Barre, Pa.	7	n.a.
Baltimore	n.a.	7
	Midwest	
Cleveland	6	n.a.
Chicago	7.25	7.5
St. Louis	6.25	n.a.
Kansas City	n.a.	5.5
	South	
Dallas	3.5[c]	n.a.
	Far West	
Los Angeles	7	7.5
San Francisco	n.a.	7.5

n.a. = not available.

Note: Benefits considered are for health and welfare, vacations, and retirement. A 40-week work year was assumed for the purpose of converting direct vacation payments into percentages of payroll. In computing the average number of vacation days it was also assumed that 30 per cent of workers had five or more years of service in the industry. The "women's and misses' coats and suits" industry, as used in this table, does not include skirts.

[a] "New York area" means 10 counties containing New York City, Newark, Jersey City, and Paterson. Chicago is Cook County; Philadelphia is Delaware and Philadelphia Counties in Pennsylvania and Camden County in New Jersey. All other areas are Standard Metropolitan Areas as defined by the Census Bureau.

[b] One-half per cent was added as an estimate of the amount contributed by the employer to pay the employee's share of state disability benefits.

[c] Since there was no formal industry contribution to a union fund and no retirement plan throughout the Dallas area, the percentage indicated represents a generous estimate of employer-financed health benefits and paid vacations.

Sources at bottom of next page.

to the fact that a higher proportion of employment in the New York area is covered by collective bargaining.

In the main industries of men's apparel, the interregional comparison of supplementary benefits presents a different pattern from that outlined above. Collective bargaining in these industries is conducted by the Amalgamated Clothing Workers of America on a national industrywide basis. This does not necessarily mean that equality of wages and labor costs is achieved among different areas. But employer contributions to health and retirement funds, as well as the provisions for paid holidays and vacations, have been introduced in a generally uniform manner in unionized establishments throughout the industry. For example, in 1956, employers in unionized plants producing men's dress shirts, whether in New York or Baltimore, contributed 5 per cent of payroll to the union welfare fund and provided their workers with six paid holidays and two weeks of vacation after one year of service. This is typical of the uniformity prevailing in most union shops throughout the country.

Yet, though the Amalgamated Clothing Workers is a very strong union, it has not been able to organize the workers equally well in all lines of men's apparel or in all sections of the country. If the producers in the New York Metropolitan Region incur relatively higher fringe costs than employers in other areas, this is due primarily to a stronger degree of unionization in the Region than in some outside locations. Thus, a recent survey by the Bureau of Labor Statistics in the men's dress shirt industry indicates that, in some areas of Pennsylvania and in Baltimore, less than 60 per cent of the workers were unionized and that workers in nonunion plants had generally less extensive systems of supplementary remuneration than those in organized establishments. This is probably the case also for sportswear and other cheaper lines of men's clothing. Even in men's suits and coats—the most strongly organized industry in men's

---

TABLE 10 (CONTINUED)

Sources: U. S. Bureau of Labor Statistics, *Women's and Misses' Dresses, 1955,* Forms OWR-24 for individual areas; BLS, *Women's and Misses' Coats and Suits, 1957,* Forms OWR-24 for individual areas; also convention records of International Ladies' Garment Workers' Union.

clothing—there are undoubtedly several nonunion establishments outside of the Region which bear lesser costs of benefits than the organized plants.[16]

In women's apparel, both our own field interviews and also some made by the Bureau of Labor Statistics indicate that the higher payments of the New York producers for fringe benefits are not limited to the industries producing dresses and coats and suits. Producers in such industries as footwear, textile dyeing and finishing, and handbags and pocketbooks pay more toward such benefits in the New York Metropolitan Region than in competing areas. No nationwide patterns have been established in these industries, and there are interregional differences in the negotiated provisions which typically provide for higher benefits in New York.[17] Again, nonunion shops, more prevalent outside the Region than in it, add to the differential. The result of these factors is that employers in the relatively well organized New York area contribute sums representing a larger proportion of their payroll than do their competitors in the other areas.[18]

OTHER INDUSTRIES UNDER WAGE PRESSURE

So far, our discussion has centered on the garment industries as constituting the bulk of employment in that sector of the economy of the New York Metropolitan Region which is under pressure to find lower wage costs elsewhere. But that sector also stretches outside the apparel complex to include plants producing certain components of electrical apparatus such as capacitors and resistors, as well as plants producing luggage and greeting cards, and still other establishments which rely heavily on unskilled labor and which sell their product over a wide area. For such plants, the differences in wages between the New York Metropolitan Region and small communities in the South or New England are important indeed, though one is obliged to evaluate these differences primarily on the basis of field interviews and of general knowledge about the wages paid to unskilled female labor in various parts of the country.

This impressionistic information indicates what our data on the garment industry had strongly suggested. In these other wage-oriented activities, wages paid in areas that compete with the New York Metropolitan Region, such as the Berkshire region of Massachusetts and small Southern communities, are significantly lower than wages paid in similar types of establishments in the Region. This is true, for example, of the wages of female assembly-line workers in the making of electronic components. The wages in the Region have been estimated at 35 cents higher than in the South and 15 cents higher than in New England.[19] These wage differences put the New York producers in a difficult competitive position.

JOBS INSULATED FROM WAGE PRESSURE

Local-market manufacturing

We turn now to a quite different group of jobs—those related to enterprises so closely tied to the local market that competition with outside areas is largely absent. Here, as we pointed out earlier, the existence of wage differences among areas has no great impact on location, but their existence does need to be appreciated in order to appraise their indirect implications for the New York area's growth.

In Table 11 we examine the wages of five manufacturing industries serving primarily the local market of the New York Metropolitan Region. To be sure, not all the beer, bread, or paint bought in New York is produced in the Region. But in the case of each of these industries, transport costs, speed of delivery, or need for contacts with customers give the local producers a considerable degree of insulation from outside competition.

The figures in Table 11 show that in all of these relatively "protected" industries the Region's producers generally pay higher wages than like producers in the Northeast and South. In three of the industries—bakery products, malt liquors, and commercial printing—the Region also exceeds midwestern centers in almost every instance; to some degree this is probably due to the high degree of unioniza-

Table 11 Average Hourly Wages in Five Local-Market Manufacturing Industries, 1955

(selected Standard Metropolitan Areas as percentage of New York Metropolitan Region)

	Bread and other bakery products	Malt liquors	Commercial printing	Paperboard boxes	Paints and varnishes
		East			
NYMR	100.0	100.0	100.0	100.0	100.0
Boston	92.4	n.a.	82.7	85.0	88.1
Philadelphia	87.3	78.4	81.5	90.5	103.5
Pittsburgh	94.4	78.7	92.9	101.7	90.6
		Midwest			
Cleveland	97.0	75.8	91.5	104.5	100.0
Cincinnati	87.3	80.4	72.6	111.2	79.6
Chicago	95.4	80.1	103.5	105.6	101.0
Milwaukee	83.8	83.1	88.4	108.4	94.5
St. Louis	97.5	87.7	85.3	99.4	89.6
		South			
Atlanta	74.1	n.a.	87.3	71.0	63.7
		Far West			
Los Angeles	111.0	95.7	108.9	119.0	100.0

n.a. = not available.

Note: All percentages were derived from average hourly earnings for individual areas.

Source: Special tabulations of U. S. Bureau of Labor Statistics and New York State Department of Labor.

tion of those industries in the Region.[20] Only in paperboard boxes is the Region clearly below midwestern areas in the level of wages—and even further below Los Angeles.[21]

"Commercial printing," with 40,000 employees in the Region, constitutes one of the Region's largest employers and merits special attention. A great deal of the output of this industry serves the needs of local business and of advertising firms and financial institutions which are located in New York but carry on national activities. In this kind of printing, adjustability to quick changes and the speedy delivery of the product are likely to be more important to the firm's well-being than any savings in labor cost that might be achieved in a location distant from the customers. Accordingly, the high wage position of the New York Metropolitan Region, shown in Table 11, constitutes no serious threat to this segment of the commercial printing business.

To the extent that some of these firms produce more standardized types of product, such as routine business forms, however, the high wage position of the Region may lead to some relative decline in production. The book printing industry, which applies the same union rates as those for equivalent jobs in the commercial printing industry,[22] is a clear illustration of a broad group of printing trades for which the relatively high wages prevailing in the New York Metropolitan Region are a severe handicap to producers. But the contrast between book printing and some of the more mercurial branches of commercial printing only serves to emphasize the relative invulnerability of the latter to high wage rates.

But the Region's wages are not consistently high in all the local-market manufacturing industries. Table 12 gives a geographical comparison of wages in three local industries in the general group of metal products and machinery. Here the Region's wages are lower than those of most of the other metropolitan areas listed. The figures appear to be consistent with the results of our own field interviews, and also with the results of earlier surveys conducted by the Bureau of Labor Statistics in other industries producing metal products and machinery. In 1952, for instance, a survey of wages in the electroplating and polishing industry showed that wages in the Region's principal industrial centers were well below those of Chicago, Cleveland, Detroit, and Los Angeles. A similar study of the sheet-metal work industry, also conducted in 1952, showed wages in New York City as slightly below those of the same four cities.[23]

Other surveys in closely allied industries have suggested a similar wage pattern. In 1953, the Bureau of Labor Statistics surveyed wages in "ferrous foundries," an industry which employs about 6,000 people in the New York Metropolitan Region. Once again, the indus-

Table 12 Average Hourly Wages in Local-Market Metal and Machinery Product Industries, 1955

(selected Standard Metropolitan Areas as percentage of New York Metropolitan Region)

	Metal stampings	Lighting fixtures	Machine tool accessories
	East		
NYMR	100.0	100.0	100.0
Boston	89.8	123.5	n.a.
Philadelphia	120.3	97.7	n.a.
Pittsburgh	109.0	97.0	n.a.
	Midwest		
Chicago	110.2	110.0	118.5
Cincinnati	106.2	n.a.	n.a.
Cleveland	122.6	119.4	105.4
Milwaukee	119.2	n.a.	109.4
St. Louis	96.6	104.7	n.a.
Detroit	n.a.	n.a.	126.4
	Far West		
Los Angeles	109.1	107.7	106.1

n.a. = not available.

Note: The percentages for metal stampings and lighting fixtures were derived from average hourly earnings for individual areas. In machine tool accessories, the New York Metropolitan Region, instead of being the entire 22-county Region, is represented by eight counties of the New York-Newark-Jersey City area; for this industry average wages were computed from selected occupational earnings, and the occupational composition of the New York–Newark–Jersey City area was used as weights for individual occupations.

Sources: Special tabulations of U. S. Bureau of Labor Statistics and of New York State Department of Labor; also BLS, *Machinery Industries, Winter 1955–56,* Forms OWR–24 for individual areas.

trialized counties of the New York Metropolitan Region display a comparatively low wage pattern—lower than eight other major cities, though higher than Boston. And a 1951 study of wages in "nonferrous foundries"—an industry employing about the same number in the Region—showed the same pattern, except that Philadelphia performed Boston's role in this comparison.[24]

Why does the Region's wage position in these metal industries differ from its position in other local-market manufacturing? The explanation lies primarily in the difference between the Region's industrial composition and those of the metropolitan areas of the Midwest. In the latter areas, the local-market metal industries are surrounded by large high-wage establishments in metal and machinery products—machine tools in Cleveland; automobiles in Detroit; agricultural, printing, and other machinery in Chicago; steel in Pittsburgh. These industries are not local-market industries at all, but serve national markets. Yet they employ largely the same type of labor as the local-market industries in the metal and machinery field. Moreover, the local-market metal industries in those metropolitan areas serve the large national-market establishments there. The result is that the high-wage policies of the large plants in the national industries exert an influence on the wages of the workers in the local industries of the metal and machinery group. In the New York Metropolitan Region, on the other hand, the national firms in metal and machinery products are responsible for a relatively small proportion of the total employment, and their influence on the wages of the small local shops is more limited.

Construction and services

Perhaps the clearest illustrations of the wage patterns of "protected" industries are offered by jobs outside the manufacturing field, particularly by jobs in construction and services. Though most of the industries in these categories have to be in the localities they serve, their importance as employers of labor means that their own wages and conditions of employment affect the labor costs of other producers in the same labor market. And, in the New York Metropolitan Region, some of the service industries—for example, hotels, laundries, and building maintenance—draw to a large extent upon the same pool of relatively unskilled Negro and Puerto Rican labor on which the low-wage manufacturing segment of the New York economy also depends.

In our interregional comparison of wages for the construction and service industries, we adopted a procedure somewhat different from the one used in the manufacturing comparison. Because there is only a limited amount of competition even among different communities within a single metropolitan area, the wages may vary fairly widely between different points in such an area.[25] Therefore, in Table 13, except for the instances noted, our interregional comparison is based on wage data for the central cities of metropolitan areas rather than for metropolitan areas as a whole. The New York Metropolitan Region is represented in this comparison by its three largest cities—that is, by New York City (the five boroughs) and the Newark–Jersey City area.

The industries covered in Table 13 are the building trades, six service industries, and one ubiquitous trade, that of truckdriving. The inclusion of truckdrivers warrants some comment. Trucking is, of course, an industry in itself—consisting of firms which provide transportation service. Most of the truckdrivers, however, work for firms engaged in other lines—firms which own trucks and employ drivers to man them.[26] Why then do we consider the truckdrivers' wages separately—and in the general category of service industries?

The truckdriver plays a strategic role in community wage patterns. Because of his repeated contact with employees of other firms and because of his union's strategic position in enforcing the demands of other unions, his wage rates are likely to play an important role in influencing wages of other categories of workers in a given metropolitan area. This is particularly true of wages in the service trades and in other "local" industries where no national wage pattern exists and where the influence of other local bargains can be particularly strong.[27]

Wages of truckdrivers, it is true, vary widely from industry to industry in the same labor market, reflecting to a considerable extent the characteristics of particular industries.[28] At the same time, however, in almost all service and construction firms, truckdrivers are organized by locals of the International Brotherhood of Teamsters, and these locals in a given area belong to a joint council. Accordingly, there is likely to be a considerable amount of interdependence

Table 13 Average Hourly Wages in Construction and Services, 1955

(selected cities as percentage of New York City)

	Building trades	Hotels	Power laundries[a]	Office building services	Wholesale trade,[a] except office workers	Local transit[b]	Truck-drivers[a,c]
			East				
New York City ...	100.0	100.0	100.0	100.0	100.0	100.0	100.0
Newark–Jersey City	n.a.	n.a.	92.3	n.a.	99.5	n.a.	96.0
Newark	106.2	n.a.	n.a.	82.0	n.a.	102.0	n.a.
Boston	87.6	86.4	93.3	81.3	n.a.	105.5	n.a.
Philadelphia	90.5	77.5	83.7	84.0	94.0	98.3	92.8
Pittsburgh	89.3	109.2	84.6	94.0	n.a.	102.4	n.a.
			Midwest				
Cleveland	98.0	86.2	89.4	n.a.	n.a.	101.9	n.a.
Cincinnati	86.6	86.3	n.a.	65.2	n.a.	100.4	n.a.
Detroit	92.8	n.a.	100.0	76.0	n.a.	101.1	100.5
Chicago	94.5	91.9	99.1	115.0	102.8	105.0	99.6
Milwaukee	86.0	n.a.	105.8	78.0	n.a.	101.9	94.6
St. Louis	85.7	n.a.	86.5	76.0	96.8	97.8	92.8
			South				
Atlanta	70.0	38.1	52.9	47.0	72.4	83.5	75.1
			Far West				
Los Angeles	89.3	90.1	104.8	83.0	107.2	100.4	93.7
San Francisco	89.9	118.9	119.2	111.0	112.2	103.9	105.0

n.a. = not available.

Notes: Average wage rates for all industries were computed from occupational earnings of selected occupations. With the exception of building trades, the occupational composition of New York City was used as weights. The occupational weights for building trades were derived from Boeckh Index Tables for Apartments, Hotels and Office Buildings. Except as noted below, the comparison is with cities, rather than metropolitan areas.

[a] For power laundries, wholesale trade, and truckdrivers, the areas are Standard Metropolitan Areas, except for New York City; Newark–Jersey City (Essex, Hudson, and Union Counties); Chicago (Cook County); and Philadelphia (Philadelphia and Delaware Counties in Pennsylvania and Camden County in New Jersey).

[b] Average hourly rates for one-man bus or car operators.

[c] Excluding truckdrivers employed by manufacturing firms.

Sources: U. S. Bureau of Labor Statistics, *Union Wages and Hours* (Bulletins No. 1193, 1195, 1205); BLS, *Power Laundries and Dry Cleaners, 1955,* Forms OWR–24 for individual areas; BLS, *Hotels, 1955,* Forms OWR–24 for individual areas; BLS, *Office Building Service, 1955,* Forms OWR–24 for individual areas; BLS, *Occupational Wage Survey* for various areas, 1955–56 (Bulletin series No. 1188).

in the wage movements of truckdrivers despite the fact that they are employed in various industries. Thus, one may consider the wage rates of truckdrivers, along with those in local service industries, as a distinct factor affecting the structure and the level of wages in a particular area.[29]

The pattern of wage differences in the seven categories presented in Table 13 resembles in many ways the picture emerging from our previous analysis. The wages in New York City are generally higher than the corresponding wages in Boston, Philadelphia, or Atlanta.[30] And the wages of Newark–Jersey City are also above the wages in most other areas. The wage position of New York, Newark, and Jersey City relative to cities and areas in the Midwest is not clear. On the basis of the figures presented, Chicago and Detroit must be considered as about equal to New York in the service industries. Cleveland and Cincinnati show variations depending on the industry, but New York's wages are higher in most of the services for which figures are available, and also in the building trades. St. Louis is generally below both New York and Newark–Jersey City. Finally, one should note the very high wage position of San Francisco, which clearly emerges as the highest wage area in the local service industries.[31]

Once again, however, the comparison between areas is incomplete without some consideration of the role exercised by fringe benefits. Here, one can expect considerable variation in practices from one region to the next. Since these service industries are largely protected from interregional competition, the locus of power rests to a large extent in the local unions, which may follow some industry-wide bargaining pattern but are not constrained by it.

Moreover, decisions on whether gains obtained from employers should take the form of wage increases or an addition to fringe benefits may possibly vary from one locality to the next. The factors which determine a particular union's preferences for the form of concessions won from the employers are not well understood by students of labor economics. In some cases, an autocratic but benevolent union leadership may decide that the members will be better served if they forego some of the current wage increases in order to gain better insurance for old age or sickness; in other cases, if the union leadership is corrupt, the presence of welfare funds offers various opportunities for personal gain; sometimes the union membership itself may express a strong preference in determining the contents of the "package" to be negotiated; and, in still other cases, fringe benefits may be emphasized to afford a temporary relief for the employer, since that kind of payment sometimes need not be made immediately. But, whatever the reasons in any given situation, the interregional variations in the relative importance of supplementary employee remuneration in union-negotiated settlements in the local service industries may be quite significant.

The construction industry provides an extreme illustration of the way in which the factors discussed above can create interregional variations. The New York City unions have been the pioneers in negotiating employer contributions to various jointly administered funds such as welfare and pension funds. In addition, some unions have succeeded in negotiating employer contributions for more specialized purposes, such as meeting the employee's share of Social Security payments. The result of the apparently strong preference of the New York City unions for various types of supplementary employee remuneration is indicated in Table 14.

The variation in the relative importance of supplementary remuneration is striking indeed. The employer contribution in New York City is a considerably higher percentage of hourly rates than in most other cities. Only St. Louis, whose hourly wage rate is 15 per cent below New York's, has fringe benefits amounting to about the same percentage of wages. Newark, though it occupies the highest position in the city wage scale, nevertheless has relatively small supplementary employee remuneration. When employer nonwage contributions are taken into account, New York City, rather than Newark, emerges as the highest area in terms of employer outlay per hour worked. Fringe benefits make the high labor cost of the New York City employers still higher in relation to all the other cities.

Table 14 Wages and Fringe Benefits in the Construction Industry, 1955

	Selected cities as percentage of New York City		Fringe benefits (as percentage of average hourly wages)
	Total employer outlay per hour worked	Average hourly wages	
New York City	100.0	100.0	8.5
Newark	98.8	106.2	.9
Cleveland	91.0	98.0	.7
Detroit	90.4	92.8	6.0
Chicago	89.8	94.5	3.0
San Francisco	86.2	89.9	4.0
Philadelphia	85.6	90.5	3.0
St. Louis	85.2	85.7	8.0
Pittsburgh	84.4	89.3	3.0
Los Angeles	83.2	89.3	1.0
Boston	83.2	87.6	3.0
Milwaukee	81.4	86.0	3.0

Note: Cities are ranged in the order of total employer outlay per hour worked.

Sources: U. S. Bureau of Labor Statistics, *Union Hours and Wages: Building Trades, 1955* (Bulletin No. 1192); *Engineering News-Record* (Sept. 29, 1955); New York Building Trades Employers Association, *Building and Construction Trade Wage Rates* (Oct. 1, 1955, mimeo.); *Building Contractor* (Sept. 1, 1955).

The building-trade unions in the other areas of the New York Metropolitan Region do not necessarily follow the preference of New York City's unions for high fringe benefits. For example, in Jersey City, as in Newark, the rate of employer contributions is much smaller than in New York City. However, the size of the total "package" of gains negotiated in New York City exercises an influence on the results of negotiations in the rest of the Region, even though the distribution of monetary gain between wages and benefits may be different from that in New York City. Thus, the high total hourly outlays in New York City influence employers' costs in neighboring localities, giving the New York Metropolitan

Region probably the highest labor cost among all metropolitan areas in the United States in the construction industry.

What about the fringe benefits in the local services? From our interviews we know that welfare funds jointly administered by the union and employers have been established in New York City in hotels, some types of trucking, and certain other services. But since we lack information about other cities we cannot make an inter-area comparison of employer contributions to such funds. For some local services, however, we can get a rough indication of the relative position of New York City and Newark–Jersey City from surveys of occupational earnings and related practices conducted by the Bureau of Labor Statistics. Table 15 presents data from this source on selected types of fringe benefits paid by employers in power laundries and wholesale trade.

From these figures one can obtain only a fairly crude picture of the differences in fringe benefits among the major urban areas. The general impression is that New York and Newark–Jersey City rank comparatively high in this respect. They rank high, for example, in paid holidays and vacations. New York City also exceeds other areas in the proportion of employees covered by retirement plans—more expensive normally than insurance or hospitalization benefits. The especially striking differential in the laundry industry is largely due to relatively strong organizing by the Amalgamated Clothing Workers, which has a special retirement fund to which employers contribute a fixed percentage of the payroll.

Office workers

There is still another group of "service workers" whose compensation in the New York Metropolitan Region can be compared in a rough way with those of other areas; these are the various categories of office jobs on which wage and other data are to be had. In the 1950 Census of Population, conducted nine years before the present writing, it was found that about 1,000,000 inhabitants of the Region fell into the occupational category of "clerical and related workers." Of these, about 600,000 were women and 400,000 men. Over 10 per

Table 15 Estimated Fringe Benefits in Power Laundries and Wholesale Trade, 1955

(New York City, Newark–Jersey City, and selected metropolitan areas)

	Average number of days of paid holidays and vacations as percentage of actual working days		Percentage of employees covered by: Life insurance		Hospitalization		Retirement pension plans	
	Power laundries	Wholesale trade	Power laundries	Wholesale trade	Power laundries	Wholesale trade	Power laundries	Wholesale trade
East								
New York City	6.7	8.3	91.0	96.0	91.0	78.0	88.0	74.0
Newark–Jersey City	7.0	8.1	94.0	96.0	98.0	84.0	6.0	53.0
Boston	4.6	n.a.	46.0	n.a.	42.0	n.a.	0.0	n.a.
Philadelphia	5.5	6.5	100.0	76.0	100.0	78.0	0.0	55.0
Pittsburgh	6.2	n.a.	92.0	n.a.	79.0	n.a.	4.0	n.a.
Midwest								
Chicago	5.5	6.7	100.0	87.0	98.0	78.0	0.0	55.0
Cleveland	5.3	n.a.	69.0	n.a.	67.0	n.a.	0.0	n.a.
Milwaukee	6.5	n.a.	10.0	n.a.	6.0	n.a.	0.0	n.a.
St. Louis	6.2	6.9	32.0	93.0	32.0	79.0	0.0	64.0
Detroit	6.4	6.9	92.0	93.0	92.0	82.0	26.0	45.0
South								
Atlanta	3.0	5.9	54.0	94.0	46.0	73.0	0.0	54.0
Far West								
Los Angeles–Long Beach	5.7	6.7	75.0	90.0	79.0	86.0	9.0	46.0
San Francisco–Oakland	6.8	7.4	100.0	100.0	100.0	87.0	0.0	35.0

n.a. = not available.

Note: In computing the average number of paid vacation days it was assumed that employees have an average of five years of service. All areas are Standard Metropolitan Areas except New York City, Newark–Jersey City, Chicago, and Philadelphia (see Table 13; note a).

Sources: U.S. Bureau of Labor Statistics, *Occupational Wage Structure* (Bulletin series No. 1188); BLS, *Power Laundries and Cleaners, 1955*.

cent of all male workers in the Region and over one-third of all the female workers were classified in this general category.

Like the truckdrivers, office workers represent primarily an occupational group rather than an industry.[32] The attachment of office workers to a particular industry is relatively weak, and there is a very high degree of interchangeability of workers among different industries employing clerical help. In view of this interchangeability, and in view of the numerical importance of this occupational group in the New York Metropolitan Region, the office workers merit special consideration in our survey of interregional wage differentials.

The vast majority of the Region's office workers are employed in business units which, in the light of our discussion in Chapter 1, could not be considered as sensitive in their locational decisions to interregional labor cost differences. This is true not only of office establishments tied to local markets, but also of many workers in the central and administrative offices of national corporations. Our present interest in these office workers, therefore, is primarily motivated by the fact that their wages influence the wage patterns of other jobs.

But it would be incorrect to assume that all office operations are insensitive to labor cost differences, and that all offices in the New York Metropolitan Region are inseparably tied by economic forces to their present location. Though the executive functions of any enterprise are likely to find a location in the Region highly advantageous, the same is not equally true of routine clerical functions. This type of operation may very well be handled in a relatively smaller community, perhaps outside the limits of the New York Metropolitan Region, where the labor costs of office operations may be significantly lower than in New York.

As Table 16 shows, the salary level of the office worker in the New York Metropolitan Region—exclusive of executive personnel, of course—is not outstandingly high. To be sure, workers employed in the offices of all types of establishments, manufacturing as well as nonmanufacturing, receive higher pay in New York than they do in other eastern metropolitan areas, in the South, and in some midwestern areas.[33] But four areas represented in the table—Detroit, Chicago, Los Angeles, and San Francisco—exceed the Region in the levels of office workers' salaries on a weekly basis, the excesses running in the neighborhood of 5 to 6 per cent for office help in all industries. The Newark–Jersey City area, it should be noted, main-

Table 16 Average Weekly Salaries in Office Occupations, Winter 1955–1956

(selected metropolitan areas as percentage of New York City)

	Office occupations in:		
	All industries	Manufacturing	Nonmanufacturing
	East		
New York City	100.0	100.0	100.0
Newark–Jersey City	97.9	98.0	96.3
Philadelphia	89.0	92.7	85.8
	Midwest		
Detroit	106.6	111.5	101.3
Chicago	104.8	104.7	104.7
Milwaukee	94.2	96.3	89.4
St. Louis	94.3	95.5	92.8
	South		
Atlanta	90.5	94.0	90.4
	Far West		
Los Angeles	106.5	109.4	104.2
San Francisco	105.5	111.4	103.8

Note: The computations were based on salaries of twenty occupations. The occupational composition of New York City was used as weights. For New York City, the manufacturing office salaries used are those in local plant offices only; for other areas, we used salaries in all manufacturing offices, including such central offices as might be there. The "all industries" group is not an average of the other two categories because it includes New York central offices, and because different weights were used in computing it. All areas are Standard Metropolitan Areas except New York City, Newark–Jersey City, Chicago, and Philadelphia (see Table 13, note a).

Sources: U. S. Bureau of Labor Statistics, *Occupational Wage Structure* (Bulletin series No. 1188); also special tabulation of the Bureau of Labor Statistics.

tained a small differential below the salary level of New York City, the difference running at about 2 to 3 per cent.

New York's relatively low salary position, as compared with some other major industrial areas, may appear somewhat surprising in view of the economic make-up of New York, so heavily weighted by large office establishments. This may be due in part to the fact that office employees in New York generally work shorter hours per week than in other areas. Indeed, the difference in the scheduled weekly hours between New York and other areas is so considerable that in terms of *average hourly earnings* of salaried office workers (rather than weekly salary), New York ranks as the highest area in the nation.[34] If the shorter scheduled hours of the Region's office workers resulted in a larger work force or more overtime pay, then the weekly salary comparisons on which Table 16 was based might be misleading. However, we have presented the data on the assumption that the cost of office operations might be better treated as an overhead cost, with variations in the number of workers not responding very sensitively to fluctuations in the amount of work available in an establishment. From this point of view, the weekly salary comparisons are more appropriate as an indication of labor costs than hourly earnings of the employees would be.

A notable feature of New York City's office employment is the concentration of central and administrative offices of firms in manufacturing, finance, and other fields. These offices employ about 200,000 clerical workers in New York City. The central and administrative offices systematically pay higher salaries than those paid in other cities, such as local plant offices of manufacturing firms or branch offices of financial institutions.[35] The reason is not difficult to guess. Though a small part of the salary difference may be due to differences in the levels of required experience and skills, the chances are that a larger part is due to the office managers' incentive to maintain the best possible employee relations and the lowest possible turnover in the staff which has direct contact with the executive echelon. This suggests that a significant fraction of the employers of office personnel in New York may be quite insensitive to modest salary differences.

The salary gap between office workers in nonmanufacturing and office workers in manufacturing is greater in New York City than in most other areas. There are two reasons, we believe, for this fact. First, the City's relatively high salaries in nonmanufacturing are associated with its relatively high wages in local services. Second, in manufacturing, New York City's industrial composition is heavily weighted by the low-paying industries of the garment field and related activities, and this has a somewhat depressing effect on the salary levels of office workers in local plant offices.

As for fringe benefits for office workers, our information, as in the case of local services, is limited to data which can suggest only a fairly rough impression of the relative position of the New York Metropolitan Region. The data presented in Table 17 indicate that

Table 17 Estimated Fringe Benefits of Office Workers in All Industries, Winter 1955–1956

(New York City, Newark–Jersey City, and selected metropolitan areas)

	Average number of days of paid holidays and vacations as percentage of actual working days	Percentage of employees covered by: Life insurance	Hospitalization	Retirement pension plan
		East		
New York City	8.6	92.0	75.0	78.0
Newark-Jersey City	8.3	93.0	75.0	83.0
Philadelphia	7.8	93.0	63.0	78.0
		Midwest		
Chicago	7.1	93.0	79.0	73.0
Milwaukee	6.8	93.0	87.0	77.0
St. Louis	7.0	94.0	75.0	73.0
Detroit	6.9	94.0	86.0	78.0
		South		
Atlanta	6.6	98.0	81.0	84.0
		Far West		
Los Angeles–Long Beach	7.1	95.0	84.0	64.0
San Francisco–Oakland	7.5	95.0	77.0	70.0

Note: In computing the average number of paid vacation days, it was assumed that employees have an average of five years of service. All areas are Standard Metropolitan Areas except New York City, Newark–Jersey City, Chicago, and Philadelphia (see Table 13, note a).

Source: U. S. Bureau of Labor Statistics, *Occupational Wage Structure* (Bulletin series No. 1188).

the employers of office help in the three largest cities of the Region do not carry an unusually large burden of supplementary employee remuneration. Again, it appears that they expend a larger proportion of the payroll on vacation and holiday payments than the employers of other metropolitan areas. But Table 17 does not suggest that other types of fringe benefits are much more prevalent in the New York Metropolitan Region than in the metropolitan areas of Detroit, St. Louis, or even Atlanta.

OTHER JOBS

Somewhere between the economic activities where wage differences are critical for location and the economic activities where wage differences are of little consequence there lies a third category—a group of industries which may respond in some degree to wage differences but which do not rank such differences very high in their locational calculus.

Classifications of this sort are, of course, exceedingly arbitrary and are not to be taken too literally. Nevertheless, as we saw in Chapter 1, the manufacturers of machinery, transportation products, and chemical products, though they produce for national markets, are relatively insensitive to interregional wage differences. For many firms in such industries, the locational attractiveness of low-wage labor markets outside the New York Metropolitan Region is limited by the necessity of having a large local supply of skilled craftsmen; by the economies of large-scale production already achieved in establishments within the Region; and by companywide or even industrywide wage patterns which leave relatively little room for interregional variations in wages. Of course, these factors do not constitute a bar to a movement away from a present location in the New York Metropolitan Region, but they do tend to limit the locational pull of lower wages outside the Region.

In Table 18 we compare the wages of six industries—three of them in machinery and transportation products and three in the chemical field. The relative wage position of the New York Metropolitan Region varies, of course, from one industry to another. But,

Table 18 Average Hourly Wages in Machinery and Chemical Products Industries, 1955

(selected Standard Metropolitan Areas as percentage of New York Metropolitan Region)

	Machinery, (nonelectrical)[a]	Radios and related products	Aircraft engines	Industrial chemicals[b]	Petroleum refining	Pharmaceutical preparations
			East			
NYMR	100.0	100.0	100.0	100.0	100.0	100.0
Boston	93.2	99.4	111.0	n.a.	n.a.	75.7
Philadelphia	102.4	112.3	n.a.	98.5	98.1	99.5
Pittsburgh	111.0	n.a.	n.a.	n.a.	n.a.	n.a.
			Midwest			
Chicago	105.8	100.6	107.8	102.9	99.2	90.5
Cincinnati	n.a.	91.8	105.1	n.a.	n.a.	n.a.
Cleveland	106.3	95.3	n.a.	102.9	n.a.	n.a.
Milwaukee	109.2	n.a.	n.a.	n.a.	n.a.	n.a.
St. Louis	102.4	n.a.	n.a.	n.a.	97.3	84.4
Detroit	114.5	n.a.	n.a.	105.4	n.a.	n.a.
			Far West			
Los Angeles	99.5	116.4	96.3	n.a.	95.4	88.9

n.a. = not available.

Note: Except as noted below, the percentages are computed from average hourly earnings in the 22 counties of the New York Metropolitan Region and in Standard Metropolitan Areas as defined by the Census Bureau.

[a] In nonelectrical machinery, the New York Metropolitan Region is represented by eight counties of the New York–Newark–Jersey City area. Chicago is Cook County; Philadelphia is Delaware and Philadelphia Counties in Pennsylvania and Camden County in New Jersey; other areas are Standard Metropolitan Areas. Average wages were computed from hourly earnings of selected occupations. The occupational composition of the New York–Newark–Jersey City area was used as weights.

[b] In industrial chemicals, the New York Metropolitan Region is represented by the New Jersey counties of Essex, Hudson, and Union, where most of the chemical industries of the Region are concentrated. Other areas are the same as described in note a. Average wages were computed from hourly earnings of selected occupations. The occupational composition of the Newark–Jersey City area was used as weights.

Sources: Special tabulations by Bureau of Labor Statistics and New York State Department of Labor; also BLS, *Machinery Industries, Winter 1955–56,* Forms OWR–24 for individual areas; BLS, *Industrial Chemicals, 1955,* Forms OWR–24 for individual areas.

with the exception of the pharmaceutical preparations industry, which is represented in the Region by several very large establishments, the Region cannot be considered as a particularly high wage area in the industries listed in the table. Indeed, in nonelectrical machinery products [36]—a category composed primarily of producers of fairly specialized equipment—and in aircraft engines and industrial chemicals, the Region's wages are lower than those of most other major urban areas for which wage data are available.

In order to develop a more adequate picture of comparative labor costs among different areas, we are obliged once again to consider the pattern of fringe benefits. Given the nature of these industries, an initial presumption exists that fringe benefits do not significantly change the picture presented by the wage comparison. These industries are composed largely of multiplant firms, frequently responding to national wage pattern changes. Many of the fringe benefits have been introduced in a period of relatively uniform interregional changes in wages.[37] The tendency to uniformity of benefits such as pensions and life insurance is also enhanced in multiplant firms because such benefits are more efficiently administered by the company staff when they are based on relatively uniform provisions in various plants of the firms.[38] Moreover, some managements which do not believe in companywide uniformity of wages accept uniformity of these benefits as fair or even desirable.

Nevertheless, one dare not rule out the possibility that differences in unions and in labor-market conditions from one area to another might lead to local differences in supplementary benefits. Yet data which might test this possibility scarcely exist. Such figures as could be had are reproduced in Table 19. These figures afford four different indices of the level of fringe benefits in various metropolitan areas as they exist in the machinery and industrial chemicals industries. The impression suggested by the data is that the differences in benefits among the major producing centers are not very great. The New York Metropolitan Region is generally a little higher in its payments for holidays and vacations, but its relative position with respect to other types of supplementary remuneration is not particularly high. In one critical area of fringe benefits—retirement plan benefits—the Region's coverage appears to be relatively low.

The position of the Region with respect to fringe benefits in machinery and industrial chemicals is probably fairly characteristic of

Table 19 Estimated Fringe Benefits in Machinery (Nonelectrical) and Industrial Chemicals, 1955

(selected Standard Metropolitan Areas)

	Average number of days of paid holidays and vacations as percentage of actual working days		Percentage of employees covered by:					
			Life insurance		Hospitalization		Retirement pension plan	
	Machinery (nonelectrical)	Industrial chemicals	Machinery (nonelectrical)	Industrial chemicals	Machinery (nonelectrical)	Industrial chemicals	Machinery (nonelectrical)	Industrial chemicals
East								
New York area	7.0	7.4	85.0	89.0	89.0	99.0	54.0	82.0
Boston	7.4	n.a.	94.0	n.a.	79.0	n.a.	58.0	n.a.
Philadelphia	6.9	7.0	97.0	99.0	95.0	93.0	71.0	95.0
Pittsburgh	6.7	n.a.	99.0	n.a.	99.0	n.a.	85.0	n.a.
Midwest								
Chicago	6.7	6.7	84.0	99.0	91.0	92.0	67.0	90.0
Cleveland	6.5	6.7	92.0	99.0	81.0	87.0	59.0	90.0
Milwaukee	6.7	n.a.	98.0	n.a.	97.0	n.a.	83.0	n.a.
St. Louis	6.8	n.a.	94.0	n.a.	92.0	n.a.	19.0	n.a.
Detroit	6.4	6.6	97.0	100.0	92.0	100.0	70.0	94.0
Far West								
Los Angeles–Long Beach	6.4	n.a.	90.0	n.a.	96.0	n.a.	29.0	n.a.

n.a. = not available.

Note: In computing the average number of vacation days it was assumed that employees have an average of five years of service. All areas are Standard Metropolitan Areas except the New York area, Chicago, and Philadelphia. The New York area is the same as described in Table 18, notes a and b. Chicago and Philadelphia, for both industries, are as described in Table 18, note a.

Sources: U.S. Bureau of Labor Statistics, *Machinery Industries, Winter 1955–56*, Forms OWR–24 for individual areas; BLS, *Industrial Chemicals, 1955*, Forms OWR–24 for individual areas.

such other industries as aircraft engines, automobiles, and petroleum refining. In comparison with other areas, the Region probably ranks slightly on the high side in supplementary employee remuneration; but the interregional differences are probably not very significant. Beyond this, there is no basis for a specific statement.[39]

SUMMARY: THE REGION'S WAGE POSITION

The preceding discussion suggests the following general position of the New York Metropolitan Region with respect to the most important components of labor cost.

Average wages in the New York Metropolitan Region tend to be below those of several important manufacturing centers of the nation —in the Midwest and on the Pacific Coast. The main reason for this fact is that a large proportion of the Region's manufacturing belongs to the general category of relatively low-wage industries—garments, textiles, other light consumer goods.

However, the relative position of the New York Metropolitan Region presents quite a different picture when wage comparisons are made on an industry-by-industry basis. In the sectors of manufacturing in which industries pay comparatively low wages, the relative wage position of the Region is very high; and in the sectors in which industries pay comparatively high wages, the Region's wage position is fairly low.

Thus, the New York Metropolitan Region is a very high wage area in the apparel and related industries complex—a complex in which the firms producing the less expensive product lines rely on relatively cheap labor and are highly sensitive to interregional labor-cost differences. In most of the industries of this group the wages in the Region, and particularly in New York City, are the highest in the nation. The supplementary employee remuneration generally accentuates the high labor-cost position of the Region's establishments in many industries of the garment complex.

On the other hand, the Region's wages are generally somewhat below those of many other metropolitan areas in a number of manufacturing industries characterized by large multiplant firms, relatively heavy capital investment, and responsiveness to national industrywide collective bargaining patterns. These are the industries—machinery, transportation products, industrial chemicals—which are in the comparatively high-paying sector of manufacturing. A limited amount of information on fringe benefits in these industries suggests that the benefits are probably a little higher in the New York Metropolitan Region than in other areas, but that they generally vary little among the important manufacturing centers.

The New York Metropolitan Region is the highest wage area in the nation in construction and the highest in the eastern part of the country in the local services. In both construction and services, the Region's employers appear to carry the cost of higher fringe benefits than the employers of other areas. The Region also ranks very high in the wages of several manufacturing industries which primarily serve local markets. In some of these industries the Region's wages are higher than those of any other metropolitan area; in others they are exceeded only by the wages of a few midwestern and Pacific Coast metropolitan areas. The only major group of local industries which does not fit this high wage pattern is the category of metal and machinery products. These local industries are apparently influenced by the inter-area wage pattern of metal and machinery industries which serve national or broadly interregional markets.

No data pertaining to the fringe benefits in the local manufacturing industries are available. However, the relatively high levels of benefits in construction and services probably exert considerable influence on manufacturing firms like those in the brewing industries—that is, firms which serve primarily the local market of the Region and which are guided in their labor policies largely by local labor-market considerations.

4

Postwar Trends in Wages

The handicap of wage-oriented producers in the New York Metropolitan Region who pay higher wages and fringe benefits than their competitors elsewhere is highly suggestive of some of the likely paths of the Region's economic development. But there is an important question which must be faced. Is our picture of the wage position of the Region merely a description of a temporary situation in a quickly changing pattern of interregional wage differences? In concentrating on the current scene, have we overlooked some fundamental trends which may soon bring about greater geographical wage uniformity and thus ease the competitive pressure on the New York producers?

In our field interviews we encountered a number of businessmen who believed that there was a significant trend toward the convergence of wage levels among the various labor markets. The view that we are witnessing a narrowing of interregional wage differences —particularly between the low wage areas of the South and the rest of the nation—appears to be widely shared.[1] A number of social and economic forces are usually mentioned in this context: the migration of workers from low wage to high wage areas; the movement of industrial plants toward the rural sections of the nation; the spread of collective bargaining; the effects of federal minimum-wage legislation. All these forces are said to contribute to the convergence of the wage levels of different labor markets.

Before analyzing these forces and their effects on the New York Metropolitan Region, we must consider the statistical record of wage trends.

CHANGES IN GEOGRAPHICAL WAGE RELATIONS

Broad sections of the country

The first fact to be noted is that the main sections of the country have been moving toward greater wage uniformity. The second is that the process appears to be a very slow one.

In manufacturing, over a period of four decades between 1907 and 1946, the wage levels of four sections—Northeast, South, Midwest, and Far West—can be said to have moved a little closer to one another. Table 20 presents the only available data on that movement.

Table 20 Occupational Wage Rates in Manufacturing Industries, Selected Years, 1907–1946

(sections of country as percentage of Northeast's wage level)

	Northeast	South	Midwest	Far West
1907	100	86	100	130
1919	100	87	97	115
1931–32	100	74	97	113
1945–46	100	85	101	115

Source: Adapted from Joseph W. Bloch, "Regional Wage Differentials, 1907–1946," *Monthly Labor Review* (April 1948), p. 373. This study was based on the results of four sets of surveys by federal agencies.

Actually, as one looks at the entire period, he notices that the trend toward greater uniformity consists entirely of the relative decline in the wage level of the Far West. The trend in agricultural wages, not shown in the table, also fails to reveal any striking trend toward convergence; here the intersectional gap declined until World War I but remained about the same from 1920 to 1945.[2]

We shall have a later opportunity to discuss some of the factors which account for the slowness of the process of convergence of wage levels of the geographical sections. At this point we may note, however, that the data for 1931–32, shown in Table 20, indicate an actual widening of the wage gap between the South and the rest of the country. This phenomenon can be attributed to the impact of the Great Depression, which caused a sharper drop of wages in the South. With economic recovery and wartime prosperity, the intersectional differences returned to approximately the level of 1919.

Regrettably, no statistics strictly comparable to those in Table 20 are available for the years since 1946. But a separate study made by the writer reveals the trend in hourly earnings differentials among the same four sections of the country between 1947 and 1954. The differentials were analyzed in 193 industries for which data were available, representing over 56 per cent of the nation's 1954 manufacturing employment. In 112 of these industries, or 58 per cent of the number in the sample, some convergence of sectional wage levels took place. The trend toward convergence was slightly more in evidence when we eliminated the predominantly local-market industries from the sample and analyzed 153 industries selling in national markets. Since nearly all the industries for which data were *not* available sell in national markets, the national-market group is perhaps more representative of manufacturing as a whole. In this group 94 industries, or 61.4 per cent of the sample, showed some narrowing of sectional wage differences. These results are perhaps not conclusive enough to permit an unqualified statement about intersectional wage differences in all manufacturing, but, in view of the large size of the sample, they clearly suggest a trend toward narrowing in a majority of industries.*

❡ Region and nation

The pattern of developments in the relative wage position of the New York Metropolitan Region since the end of World War II

* The study used statistics of average hourly earnings derived from the data on gross earnings and manhours worked during the year, published in the U.S. *Census of Manufactures* for 1947 and 1954. The so-called "four-digit" industrial classifications were used. The dispersion of earnings among the four sections of the country—Northeast, South, North Central (corresponding to the Midwest in Table 20), and West—was measured by the Pearsonian coefficient of variation. The study was financed by the Sloan Research Grant Committee of the Amos Tuck School of Business Administration at Hanover, New Hampshire. All the relevant statistics and their analysis are contained in a research report submitted to this Committee.

cannot be summarized quite so easily. It is one thing to speak of broad regions of the country, another to compare different metropolitan areas within those broad regions. Let us consider first the New York Metropolitan Region *versus* other major metropolitan areas. Here the pattern of changes in the wage differences shows considerable variations from one segment of economic activity to another.

To begin with, in the complex of the garment and related industries, some narrowing of wage differences between the Region and other metropolitan areas has taken place between 1947 and 1955. This narrowing, as Table 21 shows, has not been universal. In most industries there are one or two metropolitan areas whose wages have moved further away from those in the Region during the nine years covered by the statistics. This has been true of Philadelphia in women's and misses' dresses; of Philadelphia, Cleveland, and Los Angeles in the knit outerwear industry; and of Chicago and Los Angeles in women's underwear and nightwear. But, despite these exceptions, the over-all impression is clearly that of a convergence of garment wage levels.[3]

In the other industrial groupings the convergence of wage levels in the major metropolitan areas has been either very slight or nonexistent. The limited wage data pertaining to the chemical and machinery group, data which we have not felt it necessary to reproduce here, indicate a slight narrowing of wage differences between the New York Metropolitan Region and other areas in most of the industries. There has also been some narrowing of differences in the salaries of office workers in manufacturing firms. Table 22 shows this trend—but at the same time it shows that no definite tendency toward narrowing has taken place in the salaries of office workers employed in nonmanufacturing establishments.[4]

In the group of "protected" industries and services—those that are insulated in a locational sense from interregional wage pressures—no trend toward a convergence of wage levels in the major urban areas could be discerned. For instance, in the local-market manufacturing industries the data to be reproduced in a later table (Table

Table 21 Average Hourly Wages in Garment and Related Industries, 1947 and 1955

(selected Standard Metropolitan Areas as percentage of New York Metropolitan Region)

	Knit outerwear		Men's suits and coats		Women's and misses' dresses [a]		Women's coats and suits [a]		Women's underwear and nightwear		Millinery		Footwear	
	1947	1955	1947	1955	1947	1955	1946[b]	1957[b]	1947	1955	1947	1955	1947	1955
East														
NYMR	100.0	100.0	100.0	100.0	100.0	100.0	100.0	100.0	100.0	100.0	100.0	100.0	100.0	100.0
Boston	81.2	94.5	83.2	89.0	80.8	82.2	72.8	87.1	79.1	83.7	54.9	64.4	73.6	81.4
Philadelphia	90.6	89.0	84.5	90.1	91.0	89.5	86.3	94.0	76.4	82.3	n.a.	n.a.	61.6	88.3
Baltimore	n.a.	n.a.	n.a.	n.a.	n.a.	n.a.	81.5	86.6	n.a.	n.a.	n.a.	n.a.	n.a.	n.a.
Midwest														
Cleveland	89.7	84.1	n.a.	n.a.	76.0	75.8	n.a.	n.a.	n.a.	n.a.	n.a.	n.a.	n.a.	n.a.
Cincinnati	n.a.	n.a.	80.6	92.2	n.a.	n.a.	n.a.	n.a.	n.a.	n.a.	n.a.	n.a.	61.0	76.1
Chicago	77.8	89.0	89.7	85.5	81.6	86.4	103.9	102.8	101.8	105.0	n.a.	n.a.	n.a.	n.a.
Milwaukee	n.a.	n.a.	n.a.	n.a.	n.a.	n.a.	n.a.	n.a.	n.a.	n.a.	n.a.	n.a.	67.3	81.9
St. Louis	n.a.	n.a.	70.3	81.2	57.9	72.2	n.a.	n.a.	79.1	86.5	55.5	69.1	63.5	81.4
Kansas City	n.a.	n.a.	n.a.	n.a.	n.a.	n.a.	63.7	76.9	n.a.	n.a.	n.a.	n.a.	n.a.	n.a.
South														
Dallas	n.a.	n.a.	n.a.	n.a.	46.9	58.9	n.a.	n.a.	n.a.	n.a.	n.a.	n.a.	n.a.	n.a.
Far West														
Los Angeles	100.0	82.9	95.5	97.4	79.6	85.4	109.0	98.4	92.7	87.9	67.6	81.7	87.4	87.2

n.a. = not available.

Note: Except as noted below, all percentages were computed from average hourly earnings for Standard Metropolitan Areas.

[a] In dresses and women's coats and suits, percentages were computed from occupational earnings of selected occupations. In these two industries the New York Metropolitan Region is represented by ten counties of the New York–Newark–Jersey City–Paterson area, and the occupational mix of that area was used as weights. Also, for these industries, Chicago means Cook County only, and Philadelphia means Philadelphia and Delaware Counties in Pennsylvania and Camden County in New Jersey.

[b] Note that the comparison for women's coats and suits is for 1946–1957.

Sources: Special tabulations of the U. S. Bureau of Labor Statistics and the New York State Department of Labor; also BLS, *Women's and Misses' Dresses, 1947 and 1955*, Forms OWR–24 for individual areas; and BLS, *Women's Coats and Suits, 1946 and 1957*, Forms OWR–24 for individual areas.

Table 22 Salaries of Office Occupations, 1947–1948 and 1955–1956

(selected Standard Metropolitan Areas as percentage of New York City)

	Office occupations in:			
	Manufacturing [a]		Nonmanufacturing	
	1947–1948	1955–1956	1947–1948	1955–1956
New York City	100.0	100.0	100.0	100.0
Atlanta	92.6	94.2	90.1	90.4
Chicago [b]	107.0	104.7	101.3	104.7
Dallas	95.9	97.5	90.4	88.0
Denver	92.4	94.2	91.2	90.9
Milwaukee	91.3	96.3	89.6	89.4
San Francisco	117.3	111.4	110.2	103.8

[a] In New York City the "manufacturing salaries" include only those in local plant offices (not central offices of manufacturing firms), but in the other cities the figures include both local plant offices and such central offices as may be located there.

[b] Cook County only.

Sources: U. S. Bureau of Labor Statistics, *Occupational Wage Survey* (Bulletin series No. 1188); also *Office Workers, Salaries, Hours of Work, Supplementary Benefits, 1947–48.*

25) will show that there has been no narrowing of wage differences. And in the local services there has been a convergence of wage levels between the Region and other areas in some services and a widening of wage differences in others. Here one could not see the effect of the socioeconomic forces which may bring about a greater relative uniformity of wages among various labor markets.

The postwar picture is then a mixed one. In spite of a number of deviations from the pattern, we may still say that the trend toward convergence predominates in the industries which compete in product markets which are national or broadly interregional. But the narrowing of wage differences among metropolitan areas has not been characteristic of the large group of industries and services catering primarily to the needs of the local consumers and businesses.

Our final piece of statistical evidence throwing light on the changes in the wage position of the Region is a comparison between the Region's wages and the national wage averages in seventeen industries. This comparison is made in Table 23. National wage aver-

Table 23 Average Hourly Earnings in Selected Industries, 1947 and 1955

(earnings in the nation as percentage of earnings in New York Metropolitan Region)

	1947	1955
Garment and related industries		
Knit outerwear	84.6	86.5
Textile dyeing, finishing [a]	94.8	89.7
Men's suits and coats	82.6	86.5
Men's dress shirts, nightwear	91.7	87.7
Women's, misses' dresses	74.9	75.9
Women's underwear, nightwear	82.7	81.6
Millinery	76.9	83.2
Footwear	65.4	71.8
Other industries		
Confectionery	100.0	102.2
Malt liquors	90.6	82.4
Commercial printing	87.3	87.7
Plastic materials	91.0	100.0
Petroleum refining	98.7	97.0
Tin cans, other tinware	98.4	97.6
Radios, related products	99.1	101.7
Shipbuilding, repairing	97.3	95.0
Photographic apparatus	93.9	104.4

[a] In textile dyeing and finishing the comparison is for 1946–1956. The Region is represented by New York City and two New Jersey counties, Passaic and Bergen. The percentages are computed from data on occupational earnings, using the occupational composition of the New York City–Passaic–Bergen area.

Sources: Special tabulations of U. S. Bureau of Labor Statistics and New York State Department of Labor; BLS, *Employment, Hours and Earnings,* mimeographed data; BLS, *Textile Dyeing and Finishing, 1946* (Wage Structure, Series 2, No. 44); BLS, *Textile Dyeing and Finishing, April 1956* (Wage Structure, Report No. 110).

ages of particular industries reflect the wage levels not only of major urban centers but also of many smaller communities in which industrial activity takes place. Therefore this comparison differs in its results from the comparison that was made earlier among major metropolitan areas.

Table 23 is in terms of average hourly earnings. For some purposes the use of average hourly earnings involves considerable risks. The differences indicated by such data may be due not to different wage levels but to a different skill composition of the work force. As indicated in Appendix A, we have generally refrained from relying on average hourly earnings for industries in which the skill composition varies widely among geographical areas; instead we have used other types of data to compare wages at a given point in time. In the present case, however, we are interested in the *changes* in the relation between the Region's wages and those of the nation. For this purpose the use of average hourly earnings is less risky. Moreover, some of the changes shown by Table 23 appear to be verified by wage data drawn from different sources. Though by no means providing an exact picture of the Region's wage position, the statistics in the table reflect, in our view, the general trends of the Region's wages as compared with those in the nation at large.[5]

And what are those trends? Concentrating for a moment on the eight industries of the garment sector in the upper half of the table, we notice that no consistent trend to convergence existed. What might be considered as a significant convergence of wage differences took place in only two industries, footwear and millinery. A lesser narrowing occurred in three industries—men's suits and coats, women's and misses' dresses, and knit outerwear—and some widening of wage differences occurred in the remaining three.

In the other nine industries for which national data are available for the period, we are confronted with the same mixed picture. The Region has moved further ahead of the nation in the beer (malt liquor) industry; the nation has caught up with the Region in plastic materials and photographic apparatus. Changes in the other industries appear to be relatively minor, and not all in the same direction.

The over-all conclusion suggested by the data in Table 23 is that in general there is little evidence of a systematic trend toward the convergence of the wage levels of the New York Metropolitan Region and the United States as a whole.

IMPLICATIONS OF THE EVIDENCE

The preceding discussion showed what appear to be conflicting tendencies in the postwar course of wage differences among the sections and metropolitan areas of the country. On the one hand we observed some convergence in the wage levels of broad geographical regions and discerned a similar trend among the metropolitan areas in the garment and related industries. On the other hand we found no evidence of wage convergence among metropolitan areas in the local-market industries and services; and similarly we could not discover any systematic narrowing of wage differences between the New York Metropolitan Region and the country as a whole.

Does the statistical record suggest that the forces which can eventually bring about greater uniformity in the intersectional wage structure were not operating between 1947 and 1955? Does it suggest that wage trends are subject to so many influences that we may not be able to make a reasonable prediction about the future wage position of the New York Metropolitan Region in relation to competing labor markets?

As we interpret the statistical evidence, the factors which may bring about an eventual general convergence of wage levels among broad sections and metropolitan areas have indeed been exerting their influence in the postwar period. Intersectional migration of labor, locational shifts in industrial activity, collective bargaining, minimum-wage legislation—viewed against a general background of full employment and prosperity—have constituted important influences affecting the geographical wage structure of the United States. But these influences, though they may eventually result in a greater uniformity of wages throughout the country, do not necessarily produce a continuous and progressive narrowing of wage differentials in individual industries among urban areas, or between particular metropolitan areas and the rest of the country. Within a relatively short period, say a decade, they probably cannot be counted upon to improve very significantly the competitive position of producers in wage-oriented industries located in relatively high wage areas such as the New York Metropolitan Region. This, we believe, is the implication of the statistical record pertaining to the relative wage position of the Region in the postwar period.

Our task now is to explain the reasons underlying this view. And to do this we shall discuss the functioning and the effects of each of the main forces which are said to contribute to a general convergence of wage levels in the nation.

THE MIGRATION OF LABOR

Long-run trends

It goes almost without saying that the movement of workers searching for jobs has had a long-run impact on the labor market of the New York Metropolitan Region. Historically, however, the most important influence was exerted by the influx of immigrants from overseas rather than migration from the low wage areas of the United States.

Even at the peak of immigration from Europe in the early 1900's, the skilled workers in industries like printing, construction, machinery, and foundries commanded higher wages in New York City and Newark than in other cities on the eastern seaboard.[6] And one can easily assume that the New York wages in these industries must also have been much higher than those prevailing in the small towns and rural areas of the East.[7] Even at its peak, then, immigration did not have the effect of reducing the general wage levels of the New York area to those of potentially competitive locations elsewhere. But what immigration did was to provide New York with an incremental pool of cheap labor particularly well suited for employment in certain labor-intensive industries, notably the garment trades.

The immigration happened to coincide with tremendous growth of an urban wage-earning population in the United States, a population with substantial demand for ready-made clothing. The New York immigrants of the period from 1880 to about 1910—mostly Jews from Eastern Europe and Italians from the impoverished south of Italy—provided labor which was necessary for factory production of garments. The wages which the immigrants received were sufficiently low to permit production of clothing for the mass market of urban workers.

To be sure, the immigrant wages were not lower than those paid to farmers' wives and daughters who sewed garments at home to supplement family incomes.[8] But, unlike the native girls on Pennsylvania farms, the immigrants—both male and female—constituted a regular work force whose livelihood depended entirely on their wages and who were permanently attached to the industry. Such a work force was necessary for modern factory production based on the subdivision of tasks. So long as transportation to and communication with rural America was difficult, and so long as the needlework of farmers' wives and daughters was only a part-time occupation, the rural work force could not be counted upon to provide a basis for factory production, even production in the cheaper lines of garments.

While immigration continued, the growth of garment trade in New York City did not impose any strain upon the labor resources of the area. Each shipload of new arrivals provided labor which started at the bottom of the pay scale and in the cheapest lines of production.[9] Meanwhile immigrants who had arrived earlier were advancing in skills, and they were increasing their wages by moving to higher priced branches of the industries.

The unique position of the garment worker in New York's economy of that period is suggested by the figures in Table 24. Even though New York was a high wage area in general, its garment wages were lower than those in other cities. This circumstance can be partly explained by the fact that New York manufactured clothing of cheaper quality than Chicago or Rochester. But the very fact that such cheap clothing could be manufactured in New York implies the presence of labor which accepted relatively low wages.

World War I and the restrictions on immigration applied in the 1920's put a stop to the influx of workers ready to start at the bottom of the New York wage hierarchy. These developments cut off the labor supply for those branches of the clothing industry which pro-

Table 24 Average Hourly Wages of Sewing Machine Operators for Clothing Produced in Factories, 1906

	Wage (in cents)	Percentage of New York City's wage
New York City	20.8	100
Baltimore	25.6	123
Boston	27.8	134
Buffalo	27.6	133
Chicago	31.0	149
Louisville	27.9	134
Philadelphia	21.3	102
Rochester	22.9	110

Source: U. S. Department of Commerce and Labor, *Bulletin of the Bureau of Labor,* No. 77 (July 1908), p. 144.

duced the least expensive garments and paid the lowest wages. They had the same effect on other industries which relied heavily on immigrant workers—footwear, silk, and to some extent textile dyeing and finishing.

This curtailment of immigration coincided with the beginning of a continuous decline of agriculture as a source of gainful employment. And it would thus appear that the stage was now set for a wave of labor migration within the country, migration which could bring about a considerable degree of wage uniformity among geographical locations. Why was such uniformity not realized? Why have the wages of the New York Metropolitan Region remained persistently higher than those of the competing low wage areas despite the possibility that workers—so it would appear—can readily migrate from low wage to high wage localities?

Migration of workers could create a considerable reduction of geographical wage differences if simultaneously a relative shortage of labor developed in the low wage areas and a significant supplement were created in the labor pool of the more industrialized high wage localities. During the last five decades the country has experienced considerable movements of labor, largely from the impoverished rural areas of the Southeast, Southwest, and Northwest to the industrial centers of the Northeast, Midwest, and Far West.[10] But this mass movement, though encompassing millions of people, has not been sufficiently large to dry up the continuing surplus of labor in the low wage communities where industrial employment opportunities were relatively scarce and where manpower relative to land resources was relatively plentiful.

The failure of the migratory movement to reduce the relative overabundance of labor in the low wage areas is reflected in the historical record of wages. The available information shows that, between 1920 and 1943, farm wages actually lost ground relative to industrial wages.[11] And, secondly, as will be recalled, in that same general period there was only a very slight convergence of wage levels among the broad sections of the country. Though migration had undoubtedly limited somewhat the upward pressure on wages in the expanding industrial areas, it had not created "tight" labor-market conditions in the low wage regions.

The chief reason for the ineffectual role played by migration lies in the fact that various parts of the country differ widely in the net addition to their labor forces. The low income rural regions, particularly the Southeast, have a considerably higher birth rate than the relatively wealthy high wage areas. Thus the supply of labor in the rural sections has been increasing at a much faster rate than in the urbanized areas.[12] The movement of labor to the industrial centers has not been sufficiently large to reduce significantly the absolute numbers of workers in the rural regions. Over the decades, migration from one area to another "has largely spent its force in offsetting birthrate differentials." [13]

One may still ask, however, why migration from the low wage areas has not been more rapid—rapid enough to pull up wages significantly in the areas from which workers have been moving and simultaneously to hold them down in the industrialized areas. The explanation appears to be as follows. Though labor migration among areas results primarily from a negative push—the lack of local employment opportunities—a *pull* must also be present. Migration takes place on a large scale only when there are expanding employment opportunities outside of the home area. The direction of the migratory movement is determined by availability of jobs and by the distance from the home base.[14] The critical point is that a mere difference in the prevailing wage levels between a distant metropolis and the home area is not generally a sufficient force to cause a mass exodus from low income rural regions. Such mass migration would be expected only if the migrants would find an abundance of jobs waiting for them in the distant labor market of the Northeast or the Midwest. But even in such times as the post-World War II period of prosperity, major urban areas have had pools of transitionally unemployed, pools partly replenished by recent arrivals from rural areas.[15] In such circumstances a move to a distant city, costly and disruptive to personal relations in any case, involves a further risk of at least temporary unemployment. The prospect of searching for jobs in the unfamiliar surroundings of a strange city is ordinarily so forbidding that only a relatively small minority of potential migrants are willing to face it. Accordingly, except in periods of utmost labor shortage, the conditions which would stimulate a mass migration out of the low wage areas—a mass migration on so large a scale as significantly to reduce the labor supply in such areas—simply do not exist.

When employment opportunities in the high wage areas are growing with extreme rapidity, a large fraction of the growing labor supply of the rural regions may migrate to the industrialized centers. Under more normal conditions the local labor distributes itself in different directions. Some younger workers stay on the farms, thus depressing farm wages to a certain extent and creating a potential source of cheap labor for a plant which would locate in a rural region. Other workers look for employment in the neighboring communities. And, finally, still other workers migrate to the major urban areas located within a relatively short distance from home. Thus under normal circumstances a very large part of the rural labor supply, instead of moving to the high wage areas, supplements the relatively low wage labor markets of rural communities and larger cities located within low income regions.

Migration during world war II

Yet there have been periods of marked labor shortage in recent decades, notably during the years of World War II. During this period, particularly during the years of full mobilization, 1943 to 1945, some narrowing of wage differentials did indeed take place. Millions of workers moved in this period from rural communities to urban centers and from low wage metropolitan areas to the relatively high wage industrial centers of the Midwest and Far West. Areas in which wages were the lowest in 1943 showed the largest percentage increase during the succeeding two years. The increases were also proportionately greatest in areas from which population was moving.[16] Undoubtedly the National War Labor Board, whose policy had the effect of permitting greater wage increases in low wage than in high wage areas, contributed to the general convergence of wage levels; but the main reason lay in the rapid shifts of labor supply. Relatively low wage areas such as Atlanta experienced local shortages of labor and were unable to draw sufficiently upon the normal reservoir of workers from the rural counties surrounding them. In an effort to keep their workers and attract new ones, they had to institute wage levels more closely approaching those in the higher wage areas, where there was more war production and where employment opportunities were expanding generally much faster than in the low wage areas.[17]

The experience of the 1943–1945 period proved that, when there is unusually rapid expansion of employment in the high wage labor markets, migration can contribute to an accelerated reduction of wage differences. But the postwar years demonstrated once more that this force operates powerfully and rapidly in extreme circumstances only.

The postwar period

The years from 1947 to 1955 were especially suitable for testing the question whether migration would significantly narrow wage differentials under more normal conditions. Except for a few "stranded communities" like Scranton, Pennsylvania, and Fall River, Massachusetts, full employment existed practically everywhere. The opportunity to find jobs at higher wages in the industrialized areas was more favorable than it had been in any other peacetime period in recent history. A considerable amount of labor migration must have taken place in these years, as indicated by the rapid population rise of the Pacific states and the relative decline of Alabama, Mississippi, and other rural states in which high birth rates prevail. This migration probably contributed to the intersectional convergence of wage levels which we mentioned earlier. But our statistical data do not suggest a drastic change in the geographical wage structure of the country during this period—certainly not a change of the dimension which could result from a rapid labor movement to the high wage industrialized areas.

The fact that migration did not cause significant shortages of labor in the relatively low wage areas is indicated in Table 25. This table gives statistics pertaining to local-market manufacturing industries in selected metropolitan areas. We have already mentioned that no convergence of wage levels has taken place in this industrial group, but we deferred the statistical evidence in order to present it in the context of migration. It should be noted that the wages of the two relatively low wage areas, Atlanta and Boston, have increased in most instances at a slower rate than those of the New York Metropolitan Region. It is true that all the areas in Table 25 are themselves relatively high wage labor markets in the broad regions in which they are located. Nevertheless, as the experience of the wartime period indicated, these areas are not immune to the wage-converging effects of major migration to high wage centers. Had large-scale migration taken place, both Atlanta and Boston would have felt its impact in the more rapidly rising wage levels of their local industries. Apparently the postwar expansion of employment opportunities in the high wage areas was not sufficiently great to cause migratory movements which would reduce the supply of labor in the low wage communities.[18]

Table 25 Average Hourly Wages in Selected Local-Market Manufacturing Industries, 1947 and 1955

(selected Standard Metropolitan Areas as percentage of New York Metropolitan Region)

	Bread and other bakery products		Malt liquors		Paperboard boxes		Commercial printing		Paints and varnishes	
	1947	1955	1947	1955	1947	1955	1947	1955	1947	1955
					East					
NYMR	100.0	100.0	100.0	100.0	100.0	100.0	100.0	100.0	100.0	100.0
Boston	81.5	92.4	n.a.	n.a.	88.8	84.9	83.8	82.6	92.2	88.1
Philadelphia	71.5	87.3	94.7	78.4	92.2	90.5	76.9	81.5	101.6	103.5
Pittsburgh	92.3	94.4	91.2	78.7	93.1	101.7	92.5	92.3	89.1	90.5
					Midwest					
Cleveland	76.1	96.9	94.7	75.7	104.3	104.5	87.3	91.5	100.8	100.0
Cincinnati	93.1	87.3	86.5	80.4	100.0	111.2	69.3	72.6	84.4	79.6
Chicago	103.8	95.4	100.6	80.1	100.0	105.6	95.9	103.5	106.3	101.0
Milwaukee	80.0	83.8	91.8	83.1	94.8	108.4	85.0	88.4	93.0	94.5
St. Louis	90.0	97.5	91.8	87.8	90.5	99.4	74.6	88.4	97.7	89.5
					South					
Atlanta	77.7	74.1	n.a.	n.a.	82.8	70.9	83.2	87.3	n.a.	n.a.
					Far West					
Los Angeles	120.0	110.7	n.a.	n.a.	119.8	119.0	101.1	108.9	99.2	100.0

n.a. = not available.

Note: All percentages computed from average hourly earnings.

Sources: Special tabulations of the U. S. Bureau of Labor Statistics and the New York State Department of Labor.

Secondary labor force and stranded areas

The implication of the preceding discussion is that many workers would have migrated to high wage regions in the postwar period if the employment opportunities in such regions had been expanding more rapidly. But the cheap labor supply of rural areas and small communities located beyond the commuting range of a metropolitan area is composed also of another category of workers—a category which normally could not be expected to move to high wage urbanized areas even in periods when employment opportunities there were increasing rapidly. This group, usually termed a "secondary labor force," is composed largely of wives and daughters of primary breadwinners.[19] The chief characteristic of these workers is that they are intermittently in the labor force. They may enter the labor force when jobs are available but then withdraw from it when the jobs immediately at hand disappear. Above all, they do not pursue job opportunities from one location to another. For a wide variety of relatively light and routine jobs, such as those in the manufacture of shoes, textiles, and garments, this group constitutes a suitable and cheap source of labor supply.

The comparative abundance of the secondary labor force in smaller nonmetropolitan communities can be explained in the following way. Participation in any labor force is to some extent determined by the availability of job openings, and therefore many potential workers enter the labor force only as local opportunities for employment are created. Generally speaking, small nonmetropolitan communities, in comparison with large metropolitan areas, have little industrial diversification and offer few alternative job opportunities. As a result, the rate of labor-force participation in these nonmetropolitan areas is likely to be relatively low.[20] But when a significant change in labor demand takes place—for instance the establishment of a new dress manufacturing shop or a shoe factory—there is a change in the local rate of labor-force participation. The increase in the demand for labor draws a large proportion of secondary workers into the labor force. Married women who have previously felt a need for an additional family income obtain jobs in the newly located plant. In this way the labor supply of a small community actually expands in response to the increased demand. This expansion, moreover, can apparently be quite sizeable. For example, according to a study of four small areas in Illinois and Missouri, 57 per cent of the women workers in the local shoe plants could be classified as belonging to the secondary labor force. Among all the workers recruited by a newly established shoe factory in one of these areas, 48 per cent were not only members of the secondary labor force but had never been in the labor force before they were hired.[21]

The importance of these secondary workers as a source of cheap labor is particularly evident in the so-called "stranded areas" of

Massachusetts, New Hampshire, and Pennsylvania—communities which have suffered a rapid decline of local employment opportunities because of the migration of textile mills, the closing of shoe plants, or the abandonment of coal mines.[22] The potential labor supply of such areas consists to a significant extent of large numbers of wives and daughters of partly employed or poorly paid local workers. This group is not prone to move to higher wage areas in search of employment opportunities. Family connections, age, and what is left of the employment of the man of the house tie them to the depressed communities. Thus, unless there is a major movement of industrial plants into such areas, we should not expect and do not ordinarily observe any pressure on the labor supply in these communities.

Migration and the wage position of the region

All this helps us to understand why the general gap between wages in the New York Metropolitan Region and wages in low wage areas has not narrowed in the postwar period. The main point is that even in a period of general prosperity, interregional migration has not created relative scarcities of labor supply in the low wage communities which compete with the Region in some industries and has not led to a significant convergence of wage levels between the Region and those communities.

However, in developing our understanding of the Region's wage position as affected by migration, we cannot limit our analysis to the broad migratory movements of the country. For the New York Metropolitan Region has been affected by a migrational pattern peculiar to itself. Puerto Rican immigrants have added an element to the labor supply which could possibly affect the Region's wage position in the nation.

In its basic features, Puerto Rican migration appears to be very similar to other instances in which labor has moved in response to expanding economic opportunities in industrialized areas. Unemployment or underemployment at home and the availability of jobs in New York or other cities are the chief factors motivating thousands of people who undertake the trip from San Juan to the continental airports. As in other geographical shifts of labor, such as those from the South to the northern industrial centers, the rate of the Puerto Rican migration appears to be sensitive to the expansion and contraction of employment opportunities on the continent.[23] Moreover, Puerto Rican migration resembles other migratory movements in still another way. Though the wage differences between the island and the continental industrial areas are substantial, only a small portion of the Puerto Rican population undertakes the journey. The lack of assurance that a job in New York will be found quickly, the potential disruption of community ties, the uncertainties involved in adjusting to the environment of a strange city—all these factors put a limit on the number of migrants.

Nevertheless, the Puerto Ricans constitute a sizeable bloc of relatively cheap labor. Mainly as a result of migration between 1946 and 1956, when the net in-movement averaged about 33,000 per year, Puerto Ricans now number more than half a million in the New York Metropolitan Region. Their rate of participation in the labor force does not differ markedly from that of the Region's total population, though Puerto Rican women do have a lower rate of labor-force participation than Negro women.

To gauge the impact of this new source of cheap labor supply on the wages of the Region, it will be useful to compare the wage trends of industries in which Puerto Ricans are employed with those of the industries in which they play no role. Anticipating for a moment our next chapter, in which we shall deal with the internal wage structure of the Region, we can make a number of such comparisons. In several New York services and industries which Puerto Ricans have entered in fairly significant numbers—including hotels, restaurants, the cleaning of office buildings, and the manufacture of paperboard boxes, paints and varnishes, toilet preparations, and radios—wages between 1947 and 1955 have risen about as much as, and sometimes more than, those of other industries in the Region. Such wages also have risen about as much as the wages of the same services and industries in other metropolitan areas. On the other hand, in the garment and related industries—a sector which employs large numbers of Puerto Ricans in the New York Metropolitan Region—wage increases have lagged behind those of the rest of the Region's economy. On the whole, garment wages between 1947 and 1955 increased somewhat less in the Region than in other metropolitan areas, though not less than they increased in the country as a whole.

This record suggests that the growing Puerto Rican participation in the work force of the garment industries is not the sole explanation of the relatively slow rate of garment wage increases as compared with those of other industries in the Region. This lag must be associated with other factors too—notably with the pressure of outside competition and with changes in demand in favor of relatively cheap, informal clothing. However, the availability of Puerto Rican labor undoubtedly made the lag possible. In this limited sense the Puerto Rican migration has to some extent slowed the upward movement of the Region's wages.

It should not surprise us that what appears to some residents of New York City as a veritable flood of Puerto Rican migration has had only this selective impact on the Region's wages. From 1946 to 1956 the migration added only about 13,000 persons a year, on the average, to the labor force of the New York Metropolitan Region. This is a tiny fraction of the approximately seven million people in the Region's labor force, or even of the more than four million in New York City's labor force. Though these new entrants can ordinarily be hired at the lowest wages, they obtain jobs in a variety of services and industries besides the garment complex, and they join unions and soon become integrated in the fabric of the New York economy. Accordingly, their standard of an acceptable wage soon approaches that of the generality of the Region's unskilled and semiskilled workers. Moreover, their economic advancement affects the job and wage standards of the new arrivals, who year by year constitute a smaller and smaller fraction of the total Puerto Rican community in the Region. Partly for these reasons we shall argue in the next chapter that one cannot reasonably expect garment wages to lag further and further behind other wages in their rate of increase. And, if the lag is checked, one will not be able to observe any significant effect of the Puerto Rican migration on the rate of change of the Region's wage level.

LOCATIONAL SHIFTS OF INDUSTRY

Though labor migration is not likely under normal circumstances to bring about a rapid convergence of regional wage levels, the process of convergence can be significantly accelerated by another force, namely by the expansion of industrial activity in low wage rural areas. The postwar period has witnessed considerable change in the sectional rates of manufacturing growth. The low-income South, for instance, has expanded its industries faster than the high wage Middle Atlantic states and the Midwest. At the same time certain low wage areas in Pennsylvania and elsewhere have become more important in garment-making. The expansion of employment opportunities in the low wage parts of the country has increased the competition for labor services there and has absorbed at least some of the unemployed or underemployed workers. In many areas the result must have been some acceleration in the increase of community wage levels. Without doubt, this is one of the forces which lies behind the very gradual trend toward greater relative uniformity of wages among the sections of the country.

Probably most of the increase in the manufacturing activity of the South has had little or nothing to do with a search by businessmen for locations of low labor cost. Other forces, such as the movement of industry to expand local markets and the changes in the structure of transport costs, probably played a critical role in the trend toward equalizing the "industrialization" of different parts of the country.[24] Nevertheless, the shifts of industrial location resulting from these factors do have effects on the Region's competitive position because they can ease the competitive pressures on New York producers in the labor-sensitive industries. One such effect has already been mentioned—the reduction in the relative abundance of cheap labor in rural communities and small towns. But there are also other effects. Many of the new establishments are branch plants of national firms in such relatively high wage industries as chemicals, flat glass, automobiles, aircraft, and tin cans.[25] We have already suggested that the wage policies of the firms in such industries represent some sort of compromise between an adjustment to the local community wage level and a policy of companywide wage uniformity. When such firms open new plants in low wage areas, their wage and benefit policies exert influence on the labor costs of other establishments in the same areas. Through the process of invidious comparison these policies tend to change the acceptable standards of wage levels in the vicinity.[26]

But we cannot say that motivation to find areas of low labor cost was altogether absent from industrial developments in the postwar period. To some extent the changes in the geographical distribution of manufacturing activity reflect a deliberate abandonment of high wage labor markets and a search for lower labor costs. The most dramatic example is provided by the men's dress shirt industry. In the last decade this industry has shifted quite noticeably from the Middle Atlantic to the southeastern states. The Southeast, which had only 18 per cent of the industry's work force in 1945, had 43 per cent in 1956.[27] In the same period the women's dress industry expanded in the former coal-mine communities of Pennsylvania; and the textile dyeing and finishing industry of Paterson, New Jersey, declined in relation to both the South and New England.[28] As these examples suggest, the shifts in the location of the wage-oriented industries of the New York Metropolitan Region have been primarily in two directions: toward the rural areas of the South and toward the "stranded areas" of New England and the Middle Atlantic states. The plants locating in such areas are in the most advantageous position to draw upon the growing labor supply of rural youth, and to attract secondary workers of small communities. These shifts in location therefore exposed the Region's producers to new competition based on the ability to utilize the sources of some of the cheapest labor available in the country.

The wage policies of firms in such industries as men's dress shirts are as different from those of establishments in the durable goods or chemical industries as the forces which have moved the two types of plants to the low wage areas. Companywide wage policies or industrywide wage orientation play no role in setting wages in the local plants of labor-sensitive industries. The main wage criterion is what the employers conceive to be the community wage level. For a majority of workers this may mean in practice the federal minimum or little above it.

Of course we should not imagine that the employers in the rural areas of Alabama or Missouri are completely free from competitive bidding for labor services. Though the labor markets of small communities are less closely integrated with one another than elsewhere, some outside pressures do exist. As industry expands both in rural areas and in the major urban centers of low income regions, and as some workers migrate to other areas, competitive pressures arise which sometimes lead to wage increases proportionately greater than those in the more industrialized areas. But, on the whole, firms searching for locations of low labor cost find communities and towns which have had little or no industrial activity and are relatively free from these competitive pressures.

At some future time, producers searching for locations of low labor cost will find that such opportunities have been largely exhausted. The low income regions, as we know them today, will become more highly and more evenly industrialized; their labor markets will become more closely integrated with one another; and the relative overabundance of labor in agricultural areas will come to an end. But this is not likely to happen within the immediate future. As shown by the surveys of wages undertaken in connection with the application of the Fair Labor Standards Act, there are still numerous locations in the United States in which a new employer can pay wages barely meeting the national minimum.[29] And there are no immediate prospects that the labor supply of these areas will be exhausted.

At this stage, we have all the elements for explaining why the postwar comparison between the Region's and the nation's wages in the wage-oriented industries indicated no general trend toward convergence, despite the fact that some tendency toward reduction of wage differences was evident in the Region's comparison with other major urban areas. The explanation, we believe, lies in the fact that some of the national averages have been pulled down by the expansion of industry in the low wage production areas. The wages of these areas, entering more importantly into the 1955 national average than they did in 1947, have offset the convergence toward New York's levels which was evident among the older centers of production.

Our discussion suggests then that producers in the New York Metropolitan Region can draw little early comfort from the possibility that the expansion of industries in the low wage, low income regions may bring about a general narrowing of wage differences among the various sections of the country. It is true that the effect of such shifts can be seen in a somewhat more rapid rise of average wages of particular industries in the Southeast, say, than in the Middle Atlantic states. But this is of little help to the New York producers, if at the same time more and more of their competitors locate in the Southeast rather than in Boston, Philadelphia, or even Dallas. The existence of a general trend toward the convergence of wage levels among broad sections of the country does not mean a continuous improvement of the relative labor-cost position of the New York Metropolitan Region. On the contrary, in the perspective of the next decade or two, intersectional shifts in industrial location which contribute to the trend toward convergence may bring about a worsening of the competitive position of the wage-oriented industries of the Region.

COLLECTIVE BARGAINING

Collective bargaining constitutes another economic force which is believed by many businessmen to contribute to a general narrowing of geographic wage differences. Yet such bargaining apparently exercised little influence in the 1947–1955 period in altering the relative wage position of the Region vis-à-vis the country as a whole.

And even among metropolitan areas, despite the prevalence of collective bargaining in the process of wage-setting, there has been little convergence in wage levels in many industries and services.

It is true, of course, that the interregional equalization of wage rates—or of piece rates where these exist—is widely held by labor leaders to be one of the goals of the trade union movement. But the effect that individual unions exert on regional wage differences depends on the economic and social environment in which the unions operate. In some situations, unionism appears actually to have caused a widening of wage differences between the New York Metropolitan Region and other areas; in other situations, it has been a relatively neutral factor; in still other cases, it has contributed to a narrowing of such differences. In considering the impact of collective bargaining on the relative wage position of the Region, it is important to distinguish among these various cases of union behavior.

✓ Local-market industries and services

In the preceding chapters we have emphasized that what we called local-market manufacturing industries and local-market services are largely protected from inter-area competition. In some areas these activities are unionized, in others not. In industries or services in which unionization is spotty, collective bargaining may very well tend to increase inter-area wage differences. When local employers are unconcerned about outside competition but are well unionized within an area, their resistance to union demands is relatively weak; and these demands can easily bring about wage increases in the organized areas considerably greater than those granted in the unorganized labor markets. The considerable widening of the wage difference between the Atlanta area and the New York Metropolitan Region in the paperboard box industry, seen earlier in Table 25, is probably due in part to this sort of phenomenon.

Of course some local industries and services, such as construction, breweries, bakeries, commercial printing, and trucking, are well organized in most major urban areas. But even in these and similarly organized industries, collective bargaining may produce a widening of wage differences among different localities. For one thing, the local wage policies of the unions may differ considerably. As we pointed out earlier, the local unions in these industries enjoy considerable autonomy in the national organization. Indeed, the dominant local union in a given area sometimes belongs to a different national union from its counterpart in other cities. In New York, the beer and paperboard box industries, as well as laundries, department stores, and local transit, are organized by aggressive local unions which do not belong to the same national organizations whose local unions organize these industries in other cities.

Apart from the nature of the local union, a variety of other factors having to do with collective bargaining may lead to geographical differences in the rate of wage increases. Ties between unions play a role; in some cities there is a close tie between the Retail Clerks and the Teamsters, whereas this link does not exist in New York. State wage laws and the attitudes of city administrations are also important; in the New York Metropolitan Region the unions get a more sympathetic hearing from local governments than in many metropolitan areas of the South or Midwest. Finally, there are differences in the strength of local employer associations, and these differences, too, produce inter-area differences in the collective bargaining of local-market industries.

On the other hand, there are collective-bargaining factors which push in the direction of uniformity of bargaining results in the local-market services and industries. These factors include the attempt of newly organized locals to emulate the well entrenched organizations in other areas, the use of another area's wages as a criterion of wage-setting in the regulated local monopolies, and the clearing-house function of the national union.

The essential point is that in the absence of outside competitive pressure there is room for considerable variation in the rate of wage changes in different areas even when these areas are unionized. Employers are not likely to be interested in equalization of wages among areas; and union leaders have no strong incentive to fight for it and may not have the power to achieve it.[80]

As we saw in Table 25, the wages of local-market manufacturing industries in metropolitan areas showed no trend toward convergence in the period from 1947 to 1955. Without special knowledge of the circumstances in individual metropolitan areas, it is impossible to say to what extent this lack of convergence can be attributed to union policies. We believe that in the beer industry the significant increases in wage differentials between the New York Metropolitan Region and other metropolitan areas are partly a result of the differences in the nature of local organizations. In New York the breweries are tightly organized by a militant group of locals which broke off from the Brewery Workers and joined the Teamsters. At the time of this writing, the lowest wage paid in these plants exceeds $105 per week.

The diverse influences of collective bargaining in "protected" local activities are reflected again in Table 26, which offers a comparison of metropolitan areas with respect to construction and services. In one important case, that of transit workers, there was a marked narrowing in wage differentials; here the wage-setting process in each city has been traditionally influenced by comparisons with other cities.[31] On the other hand, the New York wages of service workers in office buildings, who are strongly organized in Manhattan, have risen independently of those in other areas, and at a faster pace. The same appears to be largely true of hotel workers, who are also strongly organized in New York.[32]

In the building trades, still a third pattern appears. Table 26 suggests that wages in New York may have risen less than elsewhere. But these data do not take fringe benefits into account. Hardly any fringe benefits existed in the construction industry in 1947. Accordingly, to get a picture of the full change in labor costs, one is justified in comparing 1947 wages with 1955 wages plus benefits. The comparison is given in Table 27. On this basis, hourly outlays of New York employers increased about the same as in other areas, and no convergence in costs is apparent.[33]

What this discussion suggests is that the continued spread of unionism in local services and industries will not necessarily create

Table 26 Average Hourly Wages in Construction and Services, 1947 and 1955

(selected cities as percentage of New York City)

	Building trades		Hotels		Power laundries		Office building service		Local transit	
	1947	1955	1947	1955	1947	1955	1947	1955	1947	1955
East										
New York City	100.0	100.0	100.0	100.0	100.0	100.0	100.0	100.0	100.0	100.0
Boston	82.6	87.6	80.0	86.3	81.2	93.3	n.a.	n.a.	120.8	105.5
Philadelphia	83.1	90.5	88.6	77.5	76.2	83.6	87.0	84.0	99.6	98.3
Pittsburgh	81.6	89.3	92.9	109.2	78.7	84.6	100.0	94.0	116.2	102.4
Midwest										
Cleveland	89.4	98.0	81.4	86.2	83.7	89.4	n.a.	n.a.	110.4	101.9
Detroit	86.0	92.8	n.a.	n.a.	103.7	100.0	92.0	76.0	117.8	101.1
Chicago	89.4	94.5	94.3	91.9	97.5	99.0	110.0	115.0	119.3	105.0
Milwaukee	78.7	86.0	n.a.	n.a.	85.0	105.8	86.0	78.0	101.2	101.9
St. Louis	86.5	85.7	n.a.	n.a.	63.7	86.5	76.0	76.0	107.9	97.8
South										
Atlanta	62.8	70.0	44.8	38.1	52.5	52.9	58.0	47.0	102.9	83.5
Far West										
Los Angeles	84.5	89.3	101.4	90.1	100.0	104.8	100.0	83.0	112.0	100.4
San Francisco	86.9	89.9	107.1	118.9	117.5	119.2	119.0	111.0	113.5	103.9

Notes: Building trades percentages were computed from union wage rates for individual occupations. The average wage was calculated on the basis of the Boeckh Index Table for Apartments, Hotels and Office Buildings. In hotels, power laundries, and office building service, the occupational mix of New York City was used in computing wages from occupational earnings of individual occupations. In power laundries, wages pertain to Standard Metropolitan Areas, except for New York City and except for Chicago and Philadelphia, which are as described in Table 21, note a. The local transit percentages were computed from union hourly rates for one-man bus or car operator. The average union rates in New York City for that service were computed on the basis of data provided by the New York Transit Authority.

n.a. = not available.

Sources: U. S. Bureau of Labor Statistics, *Union Wages and Hours* (Bulletins No. 930, 933, 1193, 1205); BLS, *Power Laundries and Dry Cleaners* (1947 and 1955), Forms OWR–24 for individual areas; BLS, *Hotels* (1947 and 1955), Forms OWR–24 for individual areas; BLS, *Office Building Service* (1947 and 1955), Forms OWR–24 for individual areas.

Table 27 Hourly Employer Outlays (Wages and Fringe Benefits) in Construction, 1947 and 1955

(selected cities as percentage of New York City)

	1947	1955
New York City	100.0	100.0
Atlanta	62.8	64.9
Boston	82.6	83.2
Chicago	89.4	89.8
Cleveland	89.4	91.0
Detroit	86.0	90.4
Los Angeles	84.5	83.2
Philadelphia	83.1	85.6
Pittsburgh	81.6	84.4
Milwaukee	78.7	81.4
St. Louis	86.5	85.2
San Francisco	86.9	86.2

Note: The ratios are for wages only in 1947, when hardly any fringe benefits existed in the industry. The 1955 ratios are for wages plus fringe benefits.

Sources: U. S. Bureau of Labor Statistics, *Union Wages and Hours* (Bulletin No. 930); *Engineering News-Record* (Sept. 29, 1955); Building Trades Employers' Association, *Building and Construction Trade Wage Rates* (mimeo., Oct. 1, 1935).

an economic environment in which general wage levels of lower-income communities rise more rapidly than wages in the New York Metropolitan Region. The strong and militant New York unions are likely to maintain their relative wage position in many local-market services and industries. As we emphasized earlier, this force will exert a continuing upward pull on wages of other industries of the Region which draw upon a similar type of labor supply.

Industries competing in national markets

When firms compete in national or broadly interregional markets, the situation is sharply different from the one described above. Here, trade union ideology and pragmatic considerations go hand in hand in calling for a union policy of equalizing wage rates or piece rates. But whether such union policies are successful depends largely on the economic environment in which a labor organization functions.

In industries where collective bargaining has eliminated or significantly reduced geographical wage differences—for example, in basic steel, flat glass, tin cans, and rubber tires—the special characteristics of the industries account for the unions' success. These industries are thoroughly unionized; a few firms produce the bulk of the output; price competition is limited; there is a pattern of price and wage leadership; the investment in individual plants is large and the establishments are not easily moved from one location to another; and multiplant firms predominate.

As will be recalled, the wage-oriented industries of the New York Metropolitan Region present a wide contrast to the industries just mentioned. They are composed of hundreds of relatively small firms operating in a highly competitive market; investment in a plant is small and entry into the industry easy; and the establishments can be moved without incurring large costs. The extent of unionization varies among the industries, but in no case is it so comprehensive as in basic steel or flat glass. Large segments of some industries—notably textile dyeing and finishing, footwear, men's dress shirts, wallets, electronic components—are not covered at all by collective bargaining. In other industries, including women's dresses, children's dresses, and women's underwear, the unions, well established though they may be, have not been able during the last decade to increase the percentage of the labor force covered by collective bargaining.[34] Even in such industries as men's suits and coats, there are apparently nonunion employers in significant numbers.

Under these conditions, the task of reducing wage differences or equalizing labor costs between the Region and competing areas is not easily accomplished. It is true that nationwide bargaining and the practice of negotiating equal increases in cents per hour seem to have reduced wage differences among the major metropolitan areas in at least one such industry—men's suits and coats. Similarly, collective bargaining has probably been responsible in part for the narrowing of wage differences between the Region and the other major metropolitan areas in footwear, millinery, and women's garment industries.[35] But even this process has been slow; for example, Dallas wages are still left far behind those of the New York Metropolitan Region. More importantly still, the unions have not been able to reduce wage differences very much between the Region and isolated production centers in small communities.

American trade unions have always had considerable difficulties in organizing large segments of highly competitive industries in which business can quickly shift its location from one area to another.[36] To some extent, as we have pointed out, the problem facing the Region's producers in the wage-oriented industries is, then, that of nonunion competition. But much of the outside competition originates from unionized producers. For collective bargaining has been effective only to a limited degree in reducing differences in labor costs between the Region and these unionized outside competitors.

One reason for the limited effect of unionization in this regard lies in the difference between the environment of the Region and that of many areas competing with it. This difference, evident in the policies of union leaders and the attitudes of union members, either slows down or actually blocks the wage-equalizing influence of collective bargaining. A good illustration is provided by the situation in the Region's synthetic textile dyeing and finishing industry, largely concentrated in the area of Paterson, New Jersey. The firms in the Region compete with plants in the old textile centers of Rhode Island and Massachusetts. Though the New Jersey and the New England mills are organized by the same union, wages are higher and work loads smaller in Paterson. And, in fact, during a few years of the postwar period there was actually a widening of wage differences between the New York Metropolitan Region and New England. For the New Jersey workers, unlike those in New England, have been drawn from communities enjoying full employment, communities whose wage levels have been advancing in accordance with the wages of oil, chemicals, rubber tires, and other high wage, mass-production industries. Accordingly, they have been pressing for higher wages and have resisted changes in work assignments. On the other hand, in the depressed communities of New England the union leaders have not been under such pressure for wage increases and have been able to persuade the members to accept increases in work loads.

The basic situation reflected in this example is not confined to the textile dyeing industry. Though details vary, analogous circumstances can be found in other wage-oriented activities. In the millinery industry, for instance, newly organized employers outside the Region are not brought up to the wage levels prevailing in New York. Instead, special wage concessions are granted by the local union. The reason for this is that a relatively insecure local union does not want to antagonize a firm which has just accepted collective bargaining. Moreover, a drastic wage change may strengthen the resistance of other nonunion employers in the area. In general, then, the difference between the firmly entrenched unions of the Region and the local unions of other areas is frequently reflected in wage policies which weaken the wage-converging effects of collective bargaining.

The most crucial reason for the relative ineffectiveness of collective bargaining in narrowing wage differences stems from the fiercely competitive nature of wage-oriented activities. The producers compete both within a given area and as between one area and another. This competition among producers influences the policies of the local union leaders. In relatively small labor markets, and also in some major ones, labor leaders are sensitive to the risk that a rapid rise in wages of the local industry may reduce employment opportunities for their members and limit the growth of their union organizations. To help their local areas grow, such leaders are often willing to maintain some differential between the wages of local plants and those elsewhere. As we shall presently see, this fact is of some importance to the wage-oriented industries in the New York Metropolitan Region. Except in the matter of wages, the Region offers many locational advantages to producers in these industries, and thus it constitutes a competitive threat to other production areas.

Opportunities to pursue independent local policies in the wage-oriented industries are created by the fact that, even when such industries are fairly strongly unionized, collective bargaining is ordinarily conducted on a local or regional basis; separate and different contracts are signed either with local employer associations or with individual firms. This bargaining pattern leaves considerable room for differences in the results of negotiations among different production areas. In the past, attempts were made in some unions to introduce industrywide bargaining patterns; but apparently these were frustrated by the opposition of union leaders from outside the Region.

But the problems of labor-cost competition among centers of production are not necessarily eliminated even when the competing areas are covered by the same collective-bargaining contract. For example, some of the competitive pressure most damaging to the Region's producers originates from the women's dress factories located in the depressed areas of Pennsylvania. These factories are not only unionized but are also covered by the same union agreement as the New York shops. Yet, as shown in Chapter 3, wages in Wilkes-Barre in 1955 were 40 per cent below those in the New York Metropolitan Region. Even when we compare Wilkes-Barre shops with only those New York contract shops producing the least expensive dresses, the differential still exceeds 30 per cent.[37] To a limited extent this difference may be due to the lower productivity of the Pennsylvania workers. But this is not the whole explanation by any means. The wages have been lower in the Pennsylvania shops because the agreements negotiated in New York have been largely ignored by the employers, the local union leaders, and the workers.

A situation of this sort can exist in an industry like women's dresses partly because styles change rapidly and piece work prevails in most occupations. Each lot of dresses involves special negotiations in which the type of garment and the type of sewing operations are analyzed. The outcome of the negotiations determines which piece rates are to be applied. Though the piece rates agreed upon are listed in the "settlement sheets," they have to be applied in each shop to the particular operations there. Under such conditions there are numerous ways of escaping a uniform labor-cost policy.

In the Pennsylvania shops, particular sewing operations have commonly been mislabeled in order to apply lower piece rates; at times the contractors and local shop committees have ignored the officially agreed piece rates and negotiated new ones. The workers in many shops have never seen any of the official "settlement sheets" and have not been acquainted with the piece work system.[38]

The development of these practices, it must be emphasized, has been primarily a response to a critical economic force—the strength of the pressures of inter-area competition—which limits the wage-equalizing effect of collective bargaining.[39] Similar pressures have also affected the enforcement of the industrywide agreement negotiated in men's suits and coats by the Amalgamated Clothing Workers.[40] Here, too, the competitive nature of the industry has limited the effects of unionism on the geographical wage structure.

In substance, the influence of collective bargaining on the wage position of the New York Metropolitan Region comes to this:

In the local-market services and manufacturing industries, collective bargaining has contributed both to widening and to narrowing of wage differences between the Region and other areas, the outcome depending on the circumstances of the service or industry. In the wage-oriented industries, unionism has been largely ineffective in reducing the competitive disadvantage imposed on the Region's producers by the producers in the low wage labor markets of smaller communities, but it has probably contributed to the narrowing of wage differences between New York and some other metropolitan areas. In general, then, collective bargaining has played only a very limited role during the postwar period in bringing about a convergence of wage levels between the New York Metropolitan Region and the labor markets competing with it.

FEDERAL MINIMUM WAGES

Federal minimum-wage legislation has been generally viewed as a force contributing to the improvement of the competitive position of employers in high wage areas. The reason for this view is easily understood: the imposition of a new minimum has its primary effect in low wage areas. Besides, increases in the wages of the lowest-paid workers can be expected in many cases to exert an upward push on the wages of other workers in the plants who are earning more than the minimum. And these developments, it is thought, are highly favorable to the wage-oriented producers in high wage labor markets such as the New York Metropolitan Region.

Since World War II the federal minimum wage has been increased twice—in January 1950 from 40 to 75 cents an hour, and in March 1956 to $1.00. Any attempt to isolate the special effects of one economic force in a complex economy is bound to be risky. Yet there is enough evidence at hand, fragmentary and perhaps equivocal though it may be, to suggest certain conclusions about the impact of the federal minimum wage on the competitive position of the wage-oriented industries of the New York Metropolitan Region.

As we interpret this evidence, the impact has been quite limited. The rising minimum wage has narrowed wage differences between the Region and other areas in a few of the wage-oriented industries; but in most of the industries in this category it has done relatively little to reduce the attractiveness of location in the comparatively low wage areas outside the Region.

The chief reason for this is that the 1950 and 1956 wage minima have been too low to have a real impact in the Region's major wage-oriented industries. In the largest garment industries—women's dresses, women's coats and suits, and men's suits and coats—the wages of the great majority of workers have been higher than the imposed minima, even in the low wage areas. For example, on the basis of earnings in August 1948—a year and a half before the 75-cent minimum took effect—the institution of a new minimum would have raised the average hourly earnings of women's dress workers in Dallas, Texas, by only about 3 per cent. Yet Dallas was then, and still is, one of the lowest wage areas in the industry.

The one-dollar minimum wage of 1956 is generally considered as having had a more significant impact than the preceding minimum. Yet here, too, the effect on the women's dress industry has probably been small. Using the August 1955 data on occupational earnings of workers in two low wage areas, Wilkes-Barre and

Dallas, it is possible to make a reasonable estimate of the effect of the 1956 change in the minimum. According to our calculations, the new minimum probably increased average hourly earnings in Wilkes-Barre by about 3 per cent; the estimated increase in Dallas was calculated to be about 4.5 per cent.[41] Undoubtedly the effect of the one-dollar minimum was more significant in some of the small communities of northern Texas and other areas where wages appear to be even lower than in Dallas. But this kind of increase could not relieve the New York producers in a significant manner from the competitive pressures emanating from these areas.

It appears from the available data and from what we have learned in field interviews that some other industries sensitive to labor-cost variations were also largely unaffected by the changes in the minimum wage. Among these industries are electronic components, women's coats and suits, men's suits and coats, and textile dyeing and finishing.[42]

There are additional reasons why minimum-wage legislation has had only limited effects in reducing wage differences between the Region and the low wage labor markets. To a certain extent its impact has been lessened by the case of "learners" who are exempt from the federal minimum.[43] Much more importantly, inflationary pressures have lifted wages rapidly, making the 75-cent minimum obsolete in a relatively short time and probably diluting already the initial impact of the one-dollar minimum.[44] The men's dress shirt industry provides an example of how national inflationary pressures made shortlived the impact of the 75-cent minimum on the geographical wage structure. Prior to the institution of this minimum in 1950, the average hourly earnings of the Middle Atlantic and New England states were 29 and 32 per cent, respectively, above those of the Southeast. The introduction of the minimum reduced these spreads to 15 and 16 per cent. But four years later the wages of both areas exceeded those of the Southeast by exactly the same percentages that prevailed before 1950.[45]

And, finally, yet another factor limiting the effect of minimum wages has been collective bargaining. The unions cannot normally tolerate having the workers in organized plants receive only what they are guaranteed under the law. This would signify the impotency of collective bargaining. Accordingly, if there are unionized workers whose wages have been outdistanced by the new minimum, a wage *above* the minimum will be negotiated. Since unions are stronger in high wage areas, this will normally offset to some extent the narrowing of wage differences caused by the minimum. For example, in 1950 many small canning plants in New York City were already paying workers at 75 cents an hour, but after the new minimum was established the union negotiated an increase to 85 cents. In the men's dress shirt industry, the introduction of the one-dollar minimum, though it significantly affected the industry, touched off a union-negotiated wage increase which partly offset the initial effect of the minimum—an offsetting which, this time, could hardly be attributed to inflation. In February 1956, just before the minimum went to one dollar, the average hourly earnings of dress shirt workers in the Middle Atlantic and New England states were 29 per cent above those of the Southeast. The rise in the minimum resulted in a transitory narrowing of the spread to 14 and 15 per cent, respectively; but six months later, as a result of the negotiated wage increase, the spread snapped back to 21 and 22 per cent.[46]

Nonetheless, in at least one industry of some importance in the Region, the minimum-wage legislation has been effective in reducing interregional wage differences and improving the competitive position of the New York producers. A careful study of the footwear industry by E. R. Livernash indicates that, since the introduction of the 1950 minimum, union-negotiated increases have not offset the impact of minimum wages on the unorganized sector of the industry located in the low wage areas of Missouri and the Southeast.[47] The result has been a convergence of wage levels between the high wage and low wage centers of production and a reduction of wage differences between the Region and the national average.[48]

Of course, the full effects of the one-dollar minimum instituted in 1956 cannot yet be measured. Our field interviews with union representatives and employers suggest that the initial impact of the change was favorable to the Region's producers in the handbag-and-purse industry, considerably diminishing the competitive advantage of producers elsewhere. Initial narrowing of wage differences has probably also occurred in children's dresses, neckties, luggage, and other wage-oriented industries; but we lack the data and the perspective which would permit us to estimate the size of this narrowing or to ascertain its durability.

In summarizing our discussion of federal minimum-wage legislation, we should emphasize that the federal minima have been too low to eliminate the competitive advantages accruing to the producers located in some of the low wage labor markets. This was particularly true of the 75-cent minimum, made obsolete by the inflation. Though the full impact of the 1956 minimum cannot be ascertained as yet, it seems clear that some of the Region's major wage-oriented industries have not been affected by it in a significant manner.

SUMMARY OF THE TRENDS

The span of years separating us from the end of World War II appears to provide a satisfactory period for an analysis of the major economic and social forces affecting the wage relation between the New York Metropolitan Region and other areas. In particular, this has been a period in which the economic factors said to be contributing to a general narrowing of wage differences among the broad sections and specific areas of the country have had ample opportunity to show their strength. Yet the statistical evidence examined in this chapter suggests that no significant improvement has taken place in the competitive position of the wage-oriented industries of the Region.

True, the normal functioning of a full employment economy, characterized by the existence of strong and free trade unions, can be expected to create a long-run tendency toward the general reduction of geographical wage differences. But the fact that such a tendency exists may be cold comfort to the Region's producers in the wage-oriented industries. Perhaps the most important factor creating such a tendency is the process of locational shifts in industries, a process which "equalizes" the levels of manufacturing in relation to population throughout the country. This very process, however, exposes the Region's employers to the increasing competition of firms locating in labor markets having relatively low wages.

None of the other forces shaping the structure of wages throughout the sections and areas of the United States—migration of labor, collective bargaining, and minimum-wage legislation—has been very effective in raising wages in the low wage areas to a level approaching that of the wage-oriented industries of the Region. The persistent abundance of labor in those areas has prevented it.

To the extent that the postwar wage trends have had any effect in improving the competitive position of the Region's wage-oriented industries, the improvement has been only in relation to other major urban areas. But this effect probably has been more than offset by the relatively rapid expansion of output in small towns and rural areas.

5

Pressures from within the Region

The undiminished outside competition which threatens the survival of the wage-oriented producers in the New York Metropolitan Region is only one aspect of the problem facing these producers. Their future also depends on their adjustment to competition of another sort—competition from other employers for the Region's labor supply.

THE INTERDEPENDENCE OF WAGES

The process of wage-setting in the New York Metropolitan Region, unlike that of such areas as Detroit or Pittsburgh, is not dominated by a bargain reached in one industry or in a tightly related group of industries. On the contrary, the course of wage movements is influenced by the policies of many employer groups and unions; and, in lieu of a key local bargain with comprehensive effects, there are many influential bargains. There are, for example, the contracts in the building trades, profoundly affecting firms in public utilities and communication; the Teamsters' contracts with widespread influence in retailing, baking, and other local-market industries; and the agreements in the electrical and chemical groups, related in some degree to the national bargains in those industries. There is the office-building service contract with the New York Real Estate Board; the set of contracts in the printing trades; and the contracts of "District 65" of the Retail and Wholesale Workers Union, which organizes both department stores and a variety of small manufacturing and processing plants serving the local market.

The pattern of wage movements produced by such varied sources is characterized by considerable diversity. Yet it is also characterized by interaction and interdependence. Though the wage movement of an industry may be under the primary influence of its own particular bargain—whether in the building trades, in the electronics industry, or in retail stores—all the movements affect one another.

The interactions come about in many ways. The firms themselves, in their surveys which provide a basis for wage policy, often consider the wage changes of plants which are in other industries and are organized by different unions but which employ similar types of labor. For example, a drug manufacturing firm watches the movement of wages in firms which perform a great deal of packaging, even though many of them may be in the food industry; and firms making electrical instruments watch the wages of large plants producing special-purpose machinery.

The labor organizations, like the employers, watch one another. When a major agreement is negotiated in one economic sector, it is sometimes used as a goal by unions in another sector. This use is not merely an oratorical device practiced by union leaders. In wage-setting, as a prominent economist observed, a policy of imitation is often one of good sense.[1] The invidious comparison ("coercive comparison," as some economists would have it) of wage gains may span such diverse jobs as printing and trucking, or printing and telephone maintenance work. In some cases, unions have in their membership workers who belong to industries primarily influenced by bargains negotiated by other unions. For example, most shops producing electronic components in the Region are organized by locals of the International Union of Electrical Workers; but there are some shops in the industry which are organized by "District 65" of the Retail and Wholesale Workers; and retail workers, in turn, are subject to some influence from the Teamsters' contract. By the same token, a local of the International Association of Machinists organizes mechanics in garages, though most garage workers are organized by the Teamsters. Through such overlapping, the labor organizations of different industries encounter one another's influence in many sectors of the Region's economy.

Most important, perhaps, is the fact that many industries and firms which follow different basic patterns of collective bargaining draw upon a reservoir of the same type of labor supply.

In some cases, the influence of this factor is fairly obvious. Paperboard box plants and television plants, for example, rely to a large extent on a similar type of Negro and Puerto Rican labor. The basic patterns of bargaining in the two industries are presumably determined by different labor organizations and different company policies. But the use of the same kind of labor is likely to bring about some interdependence of wage movement over a period of years.

In other situations, the interdependence of wage movements may be reflected in a more subtle way. The relatively small shops producing specialized paper products, such as special office files, employ many unskilled Negro and Puerto Rican workers. But some jobs in these shops are occupied by skilled printing pressmen; and through these jobs the influence of bargains in the printing industry spreads into the paper-products shops. Indeed, there is a special local of the Pressmen's union which has organized many of these shops. The same Pressmen's local also organizes paper-products jobbers, and there—in connection with the warehousing operations—it encounters the influence of the Teamsters.

To be sure, because of the sheer size of the Region, as well as the diversity of its industrial composition, wages in some industries may move quite independently of wages in others. For example, collective bargaining in the chemical plants or petroleum refineries of Union County, New Jersey, can hardly exert any noticeable influence on the wage changes of Puerto Rican workers in New York City hotels. Nevertheless, wage interactions do cross state boundaries. The labor markets of New York City and Newark–Jersey City, for example, are linked by the interdependence of bargains made by unions in both areas and by the reliance of both areas upon a pool of workers who move across the Hudson River in their journeys to work.

Any concentration of activity as large and complex as that of the New York Metropolitan Region is characterized by considerable differences in wages paid for similar types of labor. Numerous studies have shown this fact.[2] New York truckdrivers in the oil industry get higher wages than their counterparts delivering fruit and produce, and the latter are better paid than truckdrivers hauling coats and suits. New York watchmen in wholesale trade receive higher wages than those in finance, insurance, and real estate establishments, and the latter are better paid than their counterparts in retail stores. These differentials reflect variations in a number of factors: the nature of competition in the product market of the industry, the relative rate of industrial expansion, the size of the firms, the skill composition of the industry in which the workers are employed. When the wage differentials are extreme, they are also likely to reflect differences in the quality of the labor.[3] The differentials exist not only among industries but also among individual firms in the same industry. In the main the differentials are an indirect result of the different abilities of industries and firms to pay—a fact also taken into account by the unions in their negotiations with the employers.[4]

Wage differences of this sort become recognized and customary in a particular market, and the labor supply adjusts itself to them.[5] Nevertheless, there are limits on the employer's discretion to deviate from the rest of the labor market. For one thing the labor market ordinarily develops some acceptable minimum rate below which only marginal workers can be hired.[6] More importantly, firms and industries in a given labor market are always under pressure to retain their relative standing in the wage hierarchy of the community.

Over a period of years, there are shifts in the standings. Some industries and firms advance in the hierarchy and others decline. For instance, an industry whose employment is declining can afford to allow its wage position to slip without serious consequences. But if an industry or firm is to expand or even keep up employment-wise with the market, the downward shifts cannot be too extreme. For just as coercive comparisons with other industries or firms affect the wage policies of managements and union leaders, so they will eventually influence the workers and particularly those just entering the labor force and choosing occupations and jobs. The price of "not keeping up with the area" tends to be reflected in workers' discontent, an increase in the "quit" rates, and a drop in the quality of new employees. In the absence of a drastic increase in the local labor supply, any firm which continues downward in its relative wage standing for a period of years will eventually experience difficulties in recruiting its work force. And this effect is likely to be felt with particular strength by firms which have traditionally occupied a low position in the wage structure of the community.[7]

The interdependence of wage movements in a local labor market is illustrated by the situation in New York City's market for office workers. Here again the salaries of basically the same occupations vary with the nature of the employing firms. Such salaries are lowest in the offices of retail establishments, and highest in central offices of manufacturing companies. In 1956, the salaries of a number of occupations in retail trade offices were, on the average, about 13 per cent below those of the same occupations in central offices of manufacturing firms. Moreover, these differences were quite persistent between 1948 and 1956, a period of full employment and strong local demand for clerical help. The persistence is evident in Table 28. This table shows the trends in the City's office salaries not only in central offices and retail offices but also in five other categories of establishments. All seven categories differ in the levels of their office salaries at any point of time; yet over a period of years these salaries have changed at almost the same rate, so that each category has retained its position relative to the others. This nearly uniform pattern is an extreme example of the interdependence of wage movements. One would hardly expect such a result among industries scattered over the entire New York Metropolitan Region,

Table 28 Office Salaries in New York City, 1948 and 1956

Category of establishments	1948 Average weekly salary	1948 Percentage of central office salary	1956 Average weekly salary	1956 Percentage of central office salary
Central offices, manufacturing	$42.03	100.0	$63.88	100.0
Public utilities	40.87	97.3	60.91	95.4
Wholesale trade	40.41	96.2	60.69	95.0
Plant offices, manufacturing	39.64	94.4	59.86	93.7
Services	39.17	93.2	58.22	91.2
Finance, insurance, real estate	37.61	89.5	56.42	88.3
Retail trade	36.66	87.2	55.26	86.5

Note: The computations are based on salaries of nine office occupations. For each of the seven employment categories the same weights were used.

Sources: U. S. Bureau of Labor Statistics, *Office Workers, Salaries, Hours of Work, Supplementary Benefits, New York, New York, January 1948;* also BLS, *Occupational Wage Survey, New York, New York, April 1956* (Bulletin No. 1188–17); also special BLS tabulation.

employing vastly different types of labor, bargaining with different labor organizations, and subject to different competitive pressures. But the example of New York City's office workers is useful in suggesting the strength of the economic forces which—generally in an imperfect and slow-moving way—compel firms and industries in a given labor market to adjust their wages to the movement of the general wage levels in the community.

LABOR SUPPLY IN THE GARMENT TRADES

The high concentration of garment and related industries in the New York Metropolitan Region, which we noted earlier, constitutes perhaps the most distinguishing feature of the Region's economy. Numerically they are of major importance, and their unions have frequently been among the most militant in the area. Nevertheless, these trades have exercised relatively little influence on the wages of other industries in the Region. Historically, one reason for this was that the Jewish workers who constituted the bulk of the garment labor pool had little contact with other industrial workers. And a second reason was that the unions' complex system of piece work did not provide a clear-cut criterion of wage gains for other unions.

Today the garment and related trades still exert little influence on wages of other industries and services in the Region. But they themselves are not immune to the influence of the Region's general wage environment. Furthermore, that influence is probably becoming more pronounced as the labor force of the garment industries undergoes a change in its ethnic and social composition.

This change has been taking place since the middle 1930's. Increasingly the Region's garment and related industries have been drawing their workers from the pool of Negro and Puerto Rican labor. The industries vary in that respect; for example, the work force in the textile dyeing and finishing plants of Paterson and Passaic is still composed chiefly of immigrants from Italy. But, in our field interviews, union and employer representatives of various garment industries repeatedly emphasized that the newer ethnic groups in the Region constitute the most promising reservoir of labor supply, both male and female. And reports on the ethnic composition of the local unions in the garment trades confirm that Puerto Ricans and Negroes are, in fact, rapidly becoming the chief source of labor for these industries.[8]

Unlike many of the Jewish immigrants around the turn of the century, these workers do not limit their employment primarily to the garment and related trades. Indeed, among the men, there is apparently some reluctance to choose jobs in the needle trades, a fact on which we shall comment later. Both Puerto Ricans and Negroes, male and female, are found in a variety of industries and services, and they are becoming a larger proportion of the employees in some of these activities—the assembly of television sets being one striking example. Our interviews show that the following industries constitute a substantial source of employment for both Puerto Ricans and Negroes in the Region.

Bakeries	Paint and varnish plants
Office building services	Paper files, envelopes
Confectionery	Paperboard boxes
Canning plants	Photographic supplies
Electronic components	Maritime service
Hotels	Television plants
Laundries	Toilet preparations
Luggage plants	Toys

In addition, the following industries and services employ substantial numbers of Negroes, though not Puerto Ricans.

Building trades	Domestic help
Department stores	Local transit
Trucking	

These lists are not by any means exhaustive; other industries and services, particularly ones which provide a source of employment to Negroes, could undoubtedly be added. But, even so, the lists show the variety of the employment opportunities which are open at the present time.

These lists have considerable meaning in view of the interrelations of wage movements in the Region's labor market. Clearly the garment sector is competing for labor supply with many industries and services which are protected from outside competition—as the garment sector is not. To be sure, some of the listed industries—luggage, paper files and envelopes, and electronic components, for instance—contain firms which are under pressure from areas with lower labor costs. But most of the industries in the list are not characterized by such pressure.

Of course, Puerto Ricans and Negroes are not the only source of labor supply for the garment and related industries. Particularly in the areas of the Region outside New York City—in Dutchess, Putnam, and Orange Counties of New York State, and in New Jersey counties such as Union, Morris, and Somerset—garment shops employ workers, mostly women, who belong to other ethnic and social groups. For these workers there are potential employment opportunities in a wide variety of industries and services, some of them in relatively high-paying plants such as those producing chemicals, electronic apparatus, and rubber tires. Thus the garment industries, whether in New York City or elsewhere in the Region, face stiff competition for suitable labor.

The influx of the Negroes and Puerto Ricans, important as it has been for the garment complex, has not prevented the industries from experiencing some difficulties in obtaining adequate labor supply. The complaint of a shortage of workers has been expressed in our interviews by the representatives of practically every branch of the garment complex.[9] The shortage seems to be due to a number of circumstances. Jewish and Italian workers have been the mainstay of garment-making in the past, but their sons and daughters have shunned the garment trades. The industries, at their going wage rates, have generally had trouble recruiting native youths, white or Negro, for many of the relatively skilled sewing jobs. And the Puerto Rican migration has not offered a complete remedy.

Most of the Puerto Rican male workers do not have sufficient skills to replace older workers of Jewish or Italian extraction. On the other hand, the relatively unskilled sewing jobs are apparently not attractive enough to Puerto Rican men to cause an increase in the immigration rate. In particular, these jobs seem to be unattractive in comparison with industrial employment opportunities outside New York City.[10] For the older generation of Jewish immigrant workers the problem of opprobrium attached to needle work did not exist, because tailoring had been traditionally a Jewish trade in Russia, Poland, or Lithuania. But Puerto Rican males, like those born on the American continent—white or Negro—show a pronounced reluctance to take jobs operating sewing machines.

The Puerto Rican migration contains in it a substantial element of a family movement.[11] This means, in effect, that relatively few unattached females leave the island for the continental United States, and that the destinations of the migrants are largely determined by what are considered as suitable employment opportunities for the male members of the family. Hence, if job opportunities for men in New York are limited, the availability of jobs for female sewing operators does not greatly increase the number of incoming Puerto Ricans.

True, some important garment industries—men's suits and coats, women's coats and suits, and women's dresses—compare favorably in terms of average hourly earnings with many manufacturing industries or services which compete with them for labor supply. In 1955, the average hourly earnings of female hand sewers of relatively low skill were $1.57 in New York contract shops of the women's dress industry; in the same year, women performing light cleaning work in office buildings were earning, on the average, $1.27. Men, too, can find opportunities for relatively high hourly wages in the needle trades. In February 1957, the average hourly earnings of male sewing machine operators in New York contract shops producing women's coats and suits under the so-called "section system" were $2.37; this is a figure considerably above what a semiskilled male worker could earn in most manufacturing industries of the Region.

But these comparisons must be considered in the light of two factors: seasonality of employment and the low prestige value attached to garment trade jobs. Seasonality in the garment trades, particularly in the higher-paying women's apparel industries such as dresses or coats and suits, means that a comparison of hourly earnings does not reveal the true difference in income-earning possibilities. When one considers both the seasonality and the 35-hour week of, say, the women's dress industry, many of the service jobs or manufacturing jobs which pay lower hourly wages turn out to provide higher yearly incomes. Though a cleaning job in an office building pays 30 cents an hour less than the wage of an unskilled job in the women's dress industry, the annual earnings are several hundred dollars more. As for the prestige factor, when disadvantages either physical or psychological become associated with certain jobs, and when alternative employment opportunities exist, a wage difference must compensate to some extent for the disadvantages. It is not only the reluctance of males to enter the needle trades; in the case of women workers, the garment industries must offer wages which compensate for the fact that jobs in a dress factory carry less prestige than, say, jobs in a television plant or a department store.

The problem of recruiting workers, though causing headaches in many branches of the garment complex, is relatively greatest in the cheaper product lines where wages are generally lower. Firms in the cheaper lines face the toughest national competition in the sale of their product, a fact which limits their ability to compete for labor within the New York Metropolitan Region. Furthermore, they must compete for labor not only against other industries but also against less wage-oriented firms in their own industries. Workers who enter an industry by obtaining jobs in the cheaper price lines acquire some skill or general know-how and transfer to shops producing more expensive products and paying higher wages. To illustrate: a Puerto Rican worker gains some experience in making the cheapest type of skirts and soon moves to a better-paying job in a fashion-oriented skirt shop. So goes the labor supply in the cheap lines of garments.

WAGE MOVEMENTS IN THE REGION

Enough has been said to establish that the ability to "keep up with the area" in the rate of wage change is a significant factor affecting the growth or even the survival of wage-oriented producers in the Region. Now we must ask how well these producers have in fact been keeping up. A fairly complete answer is provided by data showing the course of average hourly earnings in the Region between 1947 and 1955 for 44 industries and services. These statistics (reproduced in Appendix B, Table B–1) indicate that wage increases in the garment sector, which includes most of the wage-oriented jobs of the Region, have lagged considerably behind the wages of other industries and services in the New York Metropolitan Region.

The lag is clearly evident regardless of the particular industrial grouping used as a standard of comparison. Between 1947 and 1955 the median increase among sixteen industries of the garment sector was 17.8 per cent. In the same period the median increase in construction and the service industries, including office workers, was 49.6 per cent; in the local-market manufacturing industries and public utilities, 52.4 per cent; and, in a group of nine industries with broad interregional or national markets, 47.7 per cent. If we exclude the garment and related industries, the median rate of wage increase appears quite uniform among the various sectors of the Region's economy. The garment sector provides a sharp contrast with the other industries and services in the same labor market.[12]

We mentioned earlier that Negro and Puerto Rican workers have been finding employment opportunities in a variety of services and manufacturing industries outside the Region's garment sector. It is instructive to compare the 1947–1955 wage changes in some of those activities with those in the garment sector. This comparison can be seen in Table 29. The contrast is just as striking as before. In the miscellaneous industries and services which employ substantial numbers of Negroes and Puerto Ricans, the median percentage wage increase was almost three times as large as the equivalent increase in the sector of garment and related industries.[13]

How can we account for the lag in the rate of wage increases in the garment sector? The influx of Puerto Rican labor facilitated the lag but did not cause it. The chief cause, we believe, is the competitive pressure emanating from outside the New York Metropolitan Region. The unions, perceiving the problems of outside competition, have exercised restraint in their wage policies. There have been relatively few negotiated wage increases in the postwar years. For example, the 1958 increase of 8 per cent in the women's and misses' dress industry of the Region was the first general wage change in that industry in five years. Similarly, in women's coats, suits, and skirts, the 1957 wage increase, designed merely to compensate for

Table 29 Percentage Wage Increases in Selected Services and Manufacturing Industries Employing Puerto Ricans and Negroes in New York Metropolitan Region, 1947–1955

GARMENT AND RELATED INDUSTRIES		ACTIVITIES OUTSIDE GARMENT SECTOR	
Median increase	17.8	Median increase	51.5
		Services [a]	
Corsets, allied garments	45.7	Office building services	82.3 [c]
Knit outerwear	39.3	Local transit	60.4 [b]
Men's dress shirts, nightwear	35.4	Hotels	58.6 [c]
Dyeing, finishing textiles	33.5	Truckdrivers	51.5 [b]
Women's underwear, nightwear	28.2	Building trades	48.3 [b]
Men's and boys' suits, coats	23.9	Restaurants	46.2
Blouses and waists	23.8	Power laundries	30.0 [c]
Footwear	18.2		
Costume jewelry	17.3	*Manufacturing Industries*	
Fur goods	16.2		
Children's dresses	14.8	Paints and varnishes	57.0
Handbags and purses	12.9	Paperboard boxes	54.3
Millinery	12.6	Bread, other bakery products	51.5
Children's coats	11.9	Toilet preparations	49.5
Women's and misses' dresses	8.6	Radios, related products	44.9
Women's coats, suits, skirts	7.4 [a]	Confectionery	37.6

Notes: Except as noted below, all percentages were computed from average hourly earnings for the 22 counties of the New York Metropolitan Region.

[a] New York City only.

[b] Computed from union hourly rates. For building trades we used the weights derived from Boeckh Index Tables for Apartments, Hotels, and Office Buildings.

[c] Computed from hourly earnings of selected occupations.

Sources: Appendix B, Table B–1.

cost-of-living changes, was the first in four and a half years. In addition, it appears likely that similar restraint has been exercised in negotiations pertaining to piece rates.

Even though the wage-oriented industries lagged behind the rest of the Region's economy in the rate of their wage increases in order to combat outside competition in the sale of their products, they did not thereby improve their competitive position in the nation. As we saw in the preceding chapter, the gap between the relatively high wages of the Region's wage-oriented producers and the lower wages of their competitors elsewhere has been reduced very little in the postwar period. Nevertheless, despite the continuing strength of the outside pressure, the Region's wage-oriented industries cannot be expected to keep on lagging inside the Region to the same extent as they did from 1947 to 1955.

There are clear signs that the garment and related industries will become less and less able to isolate themselves from the web of relations linking the wage movements of industries within the Region. These signs can be read in the increasing employment opportunities for Negroes and Puerto Ricans in industries whose wages have been rising more rapidly than in garment-making, and in the difficulties of labor recruitment in the garment industries at all levels of skill.

The wage-oriented firms of the garment complex cannot increase wages at a significantly slower pace than the rest of the industries to which they belong. In the first place, as we have said, these firms face competition for labor supply both from the producers of more expensive garments in the same industries and from the Region's industries outside the garment group. In the second place, the realities of union politics make it difficult to follow two markedly different wage policies in the same locality within a single industry. Hence the wage-oriented sectors of the garment complex will have to approach more closely than they have done in the postwar period the pattern of wage changes in the Region.

In such industries as the textile dyeing and finishing industry of Paterson, this means following in a general way the wage movement of the high wage plants located in the Newark–Jersey City area of the Region. In the garment firms of New York City it means adjusting their wage movements to those of many local services and industries that are largely protected from outside competition.

ESCAPE TO THE SUBURBS

Ever since the 1920's or earlier, the counties in the New York Metropolitan Region outside New York City have provided an escape for New York producers squeezed on one side by competition from low wage labor markets and on the other by the high wage environment of the City. New York firms in many garment and related industries, including children's outerwear, women's coats, suits, and skirts, and women's dresses, have been moving to sources of suitable labor supply located in one or another of the seventeen counties outside the City's boroughs. To be sure, the wages of the garment complex in those counties have been higher than in the competing markets of the "stranded areas," or the rural communities of the Southeast, or indeed most major urban centers. But they have been below those of New York City. Accordingly, as the Region's producers moved to Westchester, Essex, or Passaic Counties, they reduced their labor costs and improved their competitive standing.

Is this means of escape from the higher wages of New York City still available? By moving to the outlying counties, can the Region's wage-oriented producers count on easing their competitive position in the nation?

A comparison of wage movements in New York City and the rest of the Region from 1947 to 1955 offers little comfort to the wage-oriented firms. The pattern suggests that in most of the industries which contain wage-oriented segments, location in the seventeen counties outside the City is not likely to be an important factor in easing the pressure of external competition. Though in 1955 the wages of the garment and related trades in those counties were still below those of the City, the record shows a clear trend toward convergence.

Wages in general have been rising somewhat faster in the outside counties than in New York City. In 28 industries and services for which a fairly reliable comparison could be made, we expressed the wage level in the Region outside New York City as a percentage of the wage level in the City itself, and found that the median of all the percentages was 97.6 per cent in 1947, and had risen to 98.8 per cent by 1955.[14] The difference in the rate of wage advances was particularly noticeable in the garment trades. In nine industries of the garment complex—all those for which data were available—the median percentage increased from 83.0 to 90.8 during the same period. (The percentages for all 28 industries are given in Appendix B, Table B-2.) The trend toward uniform wage levels is particularly noticeable in three garment industries which have relatively large numbers of wage-oriented producers: children's dresses, women's and misses' dresses, and women's underwear and nightwear.

The postwar narrowing of wage differences between New York City and the rest of the Region does not by itself mean that the convergence will continue. But there is another important reason which leads us to believe that a further convergence of garment wages within the Region will take place. The reason is the continuing movement of manufacturing employment from New York City into the other counties of the Region. This movement is strikingly illustrated by statistics on the redistribution of jobs in the Region during the postwar period. Between 1947 and 1956, New York City's share of all manufacturing jobs in the Region fell from 53.8 to 48.5 per cent. Though the total number of these jobs in the Region increased by about 100,000, New York City's manufacturing employment fell by over 50,000.[15]

In the garment industries this outward movement has been motivated primarily by labor-market considerations. But in other industries the underlying reasons have had little to do with labor. Instead, they have reflected forces which over a period of decades had led to the location of large plants and relatively high wage, mass-production industries in the counties outside of New York City. Though this is a book about the labor market, a few words about these nonlabor forces will be necessary to our argument.

The most pervasive of the forces has been the search for space. Small firms which are unwilling or unable to finance their own structures find more rentable space in New York City than the rest of the Region combined; but a firm which needs a large plant and separate quarters finds considerable advantages in building outside the City. For one thing, land is much more expensive in New York City than in the counties farther out. Also, city blocks are usually subdivided into small parcels, leading to formidable difficulties in site acquisition. And, finally, blocks are just not long enough to accommodate some plants.[16]

In the last few decades, technological changes have placed increased emphasis on the factory building tailored to the needs of manufacturing processes. As a result of the introduction of continuous material flow systems and automatic controls in processing, plants have tended to become low and extensive, all on one floor and therefore demanding considerably more land per square foot of floor space. These changes have increased the locational advantages of the outlying counties for new plants. They have also helped to make obsolescent many old multistoried structures in New York City.

An additional impetus to the outward trend in manufacturing location has been provided by developments in transportation. From the transport point of view, the locational advantage of the west side of the Hudson River dates back to the rise of railroads. Location in the New Jersey counties provided easy access to the terminals of rail lines leading west and south. The more recent and still continuing growth of motor truck transport added strength to the centrifugal forces because it permitted location in the outer counties, on sites further removed from the rail terminals. At the same time, the traffic congestion of New York City created an additional burden for the local plants which use trucking. The effect of motor transport, then, has been to facilitate the search for space in the less industrialized counties of the Region and to create a locational handicap in New York City.[17]

The forces which we have been describing have strongly affected the location of large establishments in many production industries, for example, petroleum, chemicals, and "hard goods." On the one hand these establishments could benefit least from the "external economies" of New York City—the economies growing out of heavy concentrations of services, suppliers, and subcontractors. On the other hand they had the greatest need for space and separate quarters. But smaller establishments have also been shifting outward, though at a rate lower than that of large plants.[18] The principal factors in this movement have been the growth of motor transport and improvements in communication.

The increasing industrialization of the Region outside New York City has had a significant effect on the Region's pattern of workers' earnings. As recently as 1939, average annual earnings of production workers in New York City were higher than such earnings in the other counties taken as a group. But today the pattern is quite different. By 1954, the average earnings of workers in most of the counties exceeded earnings in New York City, as shown in Table 30.

Table 30 Annual Earnings of Manufacturing Production Workers in Counties of New York Metropolitan Region, 1954

(outlying counties as percentage of New York City)

All counties outside New York City	118.1	Fairfield	116.8
		Hudson	115.9
		Passaic	113.6
Nassau	137.8	Essex	113.4
Suffolk	129.0	Westchester	111.1
Union	127.5	Morris	110.9
Dutchess	126.6	Rockland	108.9
Somerset	119.6	Putnam	105.5
Bergen	119.5	Monmouth	91.2
Middlesex	119.2	Orange	91.1

Source: U.S. *1954 Census of Manufactures.*

This reversal reflects the fact that in contrast to New York City the economy of the rest of the Region is heavily weighted today with large plants of the high wage industries. And it likewise reflects the fact that wages in those plants have been advancing more rapidly than in the garment complex which still dominates the manufacturing economy of New York City.

The thickening industrial environment of the counties outside the City imposes a limit on the ability of garment production to move outward without further narrowing the wage differences between those counties and the City. The wage levels of the large local employers in various communities of the Region affect to some extent the wage levels of other establishments there. As both garment-making and other industries expand in outlying counties, the wage-oriented manufacturers in the cheaper product lines will find increasing difficulties in recruiting labor at the rates they are able to pay.

Improved motor transportation will push more manufacturing of various kinds toward the very edges of the Region—for example, Orange and Dutchess Counties to the north, Somerset to the west, and Monmouth to the south. Such counties could also be considered as potential centers of garment growth, offering a possibility of tapping the sources of local female labor. But competition of other plants and the general stepping up of economic activity in these counties will put a damper on the entry of those garment producers who are under pressure to pay wages considerably lower than those prevailing in New York City.

What we have said does not imply that the Region outside New York City will experience no further growth in garment and related industries. On the contrary, for firms in higher price lines the still existing wage differentials and such nonlabor factors as lower rents and improved transportation facilities will provide an incentive to locate in certain areas. The relatively higher-paying branches of the industries, and particularly the producers of women's coats and suits, will undoubtedly find within the next decade a fairly ample supply of labor outside New York City.

For one thing, even a rapid expansion of high wage establishments leaves pockets of labor supply available for less desirable employment. In any industrial community there are some workers who because of sex, race, or other characteristics are not considered as suitable employees by the local high wage establishments. Moreover, as a result of the continuing trend toward suburban living, some of the congested areas such as exist in Passaic, Hudson, and Bergen Counties, and even Orange, will provide a stock of aged housing, abandoned by middle and high income groups, and available for people of low income, including Negroes and Puerto Ricans. The low-income concentrations around Paterson, Jersey City, and Newburgh provide, then, a source of potential labor for the garment industries.

But we must emphasize again that the wage-oriented segments of these industries cannot expect relief from their economic ailments by locating in the Region outside New York City. The supply of cheap labor there is taken up not only by the growth of other industries but also by the growth of higher price lines of garment-making. In addition, the same forces which lead to concentration of low income groups in the rundown and congested portions of Paterson or Newburgh will keep the bulk of available cheap labor in the obsolescent and rundown sections of New York City. Though improved transportation has in recent years given rise to a commuter flow of Negroes from the City to jobs in New Jersey, one can hardly expect that much commuting will be directed toward shops which pay wages significantly lower than those in Manhattan.

Our discussion of the movement of industries within the Region implies the following conclusions. The existing wage differences and availability of labor in the counties beyond the limits of New York City, as well as the nonlabor considerations, will lead to some expansion of garment and related industries in those counties. But those firms which produce the cheapest price lines, and which must compete with shops in the low wage areas of New England, Pennsylvania, or the South, can hardly count on improving their competitive position by leaving New York City for the surrounding counties in New Jersey and New York State.

6

The Wage Factor and the Region's Future

The evidence presented in the preceding chapters points to the significant factors in the wage picture which must be taken into account in considering the growth of employment in the New York Metropolitan Region—the high wage position of the Region; the persistence of wage differentials between the Region and other parts of the nation; the closing of the wage gap between New York City and the rest of the Region.

Yet the recognition of the role of these factors does not alone provide a sufficient basis for judging the relative importance of the wage factor as an influence on the future growth of the Region. For, as we emphasized earlier, the industrial composition of what we term the wage-oriented sector is not fixed for all time. Industries which were once insensitive to inter-area differences become sensitive to such differences through changes in products and changes in technology. And, as some firms already under wage pressure succumb to outside competition, the Region is being constantly repopulated with new establishments which may eventually become a part of the wage-oriented sector and subject to competition from areas with lower wages. The 60,000 to 80,000 jobs whose locational problems we discussed in the preceding chapters, therefore, comprise the wage-oriented sector of the Region at a particular point of time, specifically in the mid-1950's.

We cannot tell today what proportion of the Region's employment will be subject to the locational influence of wages in the next decade. But we are not without some guide to the future. During the several decades in which the Region has been a high wage area, its firms have been constantly exposed to outside competition based on lower wage costs. We can thus see the magnitude of the influence of the wage factor in perspective as we review the history of wage-oriented shifts in location. Such a review will require us once more to reach out from time to time beyond the limits of this volume, to bring in the results developed in other segments of the New York Metropolitan Region Study.

THE WAGE FACTOR'S INFLUENCE IN PERSPECTIVE

The high wage environment of New York began to exert its locational influence with particular force around the end of World War I.[1] The underlying reasons have been already indicated. On the one hand, the curtailment of immigration deprived New York City of the source of labor supply for its cheapest and most competitive branches of labor-intensive industries. On the other hand, the decline of agriculture created a reservoir of cheap labor in rural areas and smaller communities, a supply of labor which could now be attracted on a permanent basis to shops located outside of major urban centers.

The utilization of this labor by wage-oriented firms was facilitated by improvements in transportation and communication. At first these improvements took such forms as more extensive and faster rail transportation and the spread of telephone connections. But a more crucial development was the rise of motor transport. The expansion of trucking made possible better utilization of the existing rail facilities in rural areas. Besides, it provided direct transportation to New York from small communities located within a radius of a few hundred miles. This change was of particular importance to New York firms because it provided quick freight connections with the low wage areas of eastern Pennsylvania and of New England. And, finally, the growth of automobile ownership facilitated the establishment of shops in towns which had to rely on a labor supply living in the surrounding countryside.

These developments provided a stimulus for locational reorientation of some of New York's industries. And their effect was further strengthened by technological changes in methods of production and in administration.

✓ Wage-oriented shifts in location

In general, locational shifts in the Region's industries came about only to a limited extent through the migration of existing firms. For the most part, industrial migration took the form of the disappearance of firms or the reduced growth of firms in New York City, accompanied by the creation or expansion of productive facilities elsewhere—either in the counties forming a ring around New York City or, on a larger scale, outside the Region altogether.

The process can be illustrated by the case of the cigar industry.[2] At the beginning of the century, New York City was an important cigar-making center. Immigrants provided the bulk of the labor. The operations involved a considerable degree of skill and were carried on in relatively small establishments. Wages in New York City were generally not above those in other cities. But the introduction of cigar-making machines caused basic changes in the locational orientation of the industry.

Wages were a very important cost element in production of cigars. Even before the arrival of automatic machines, the search for cheap labor had led to some relocations in the New York industry. Such movement was largely to other counties of the Region, particularly in New Jersey. But, as the introduction of machinery eliminated the need for skills, and as immigration restrictions reduced the influx of unskilled workers through Ellis Island, production shifted away from the New York Metropolitan Region. Hundreds of small establishments in New York City and New Jersey were liquidated. Their place in national production was taken by large plants located in low wage areas of Pennsylvania and the South.

In the decades since the 1920's, the Region's employment in cigar-making continued to decline, both in absolute numbers and as a share of national employment. All that remain are small shops which employ a few skilled workers and cater to the custom-order trade in the local market.

In the apparel field the locational shifting has been more complex. The relocation of production, instead of bringing about the migration of the bulk of the industry, has consisted of a continual process of "peeling off" of particular branches of production from the body of the Region's employment.[3]

This process began in men's work clothing and women's house dresses. Both industries employ relatively unskilled female labor, and their products are highly standardized. Producing on a large scale and not governed by rapid style changes, the firms involved have no desperate need of the external economies available in the New York Metropolitan Region. At the same time, labor cost is a crucial factor for survival. As the immigration laws cut off the influx of cheap labor and as improved transportation made it feasible to locate in low wage labor markets, these industries began to leave the Region. While New York firms declined, the production of work clothing and house dresses expanded in Pennsylvania, in the Southeast, and in the low wage urban labor markets of St. Louis and Kansas City.

But the wage-oriented shifts in location have not been confined to these cheapest products. In the 1920's, New York City emerged as clearly the highest wage area in women's and children's garments. At the same time, it appeared as the highest wage area in men's clothing—except for Chicago, which specialized in quality production.[4] As a consequence, producers in other lines of garments—lines less standardized than house dresses or work clothing—began to search for locations with lower labor cost.

It is beyond the scope of our story to describe in detail the shifts which have resulted from this search. All we can do here is to emphasize some of their key characteristics. In the two main branches of women's clothing—the women's and misses' dress industry, which makes individually priced dresses, and the industry making coats and suits—the shifts were facilitated by two factors which gained in importance during the late 1920's. One was the physical separation of the actual production—the sewing of the garments—from the merchandising and cutting operations. The other was the rise of "section work," which required relatively little skilled labor. As a consequence of these developments, contractors producing cheaper types of dresses or coats and suits could locate outside New York City and still provide the jobbers (that is, the merchandisers who also frequently did the cutting of garments on their own premises) with quick delivery of the product by truck. In this way it was possible for firms to retain many of the advantages of proximity to the center of fashion and skilled labor in New York City while enjoying lower labor costs in the sewing of the garments.

As we have seen, the search for cheaper labor did not always push the garment firms entirely out of the Region. As in cigar-making, many firms moved to the Region's suburban counties; indeed, in women's coats and suits the bulk of the City's loss has been made up by employment in those counties. But the labor available in the mining communities of Pennsylvania and the textile towns of New England has been even cheaper than that available in the Region's outlying counties. Overnight by truck from New York City, these communities could maintain close ties with Manhattan's Garment Center. Under the "section work" system, the producers could employ local women who had had no previous experience in the needle trades. As a consequence, dress contractors in the lower price lines moved increasingly to these communities. The relative decline of inexpensive dress production in the Region has been accelerated by expansion in still other areas in the South and Midwest.

Locational changes in other New York clothing industries displayed many similar features. In the more standardized and cheaper branches of women's undergarments, children's outerwear, and men's clothing, the New Jersey counties of the Region gained at the expense of New York City; but the search for lower labor costs again led eventually outside of the New York Metropolitan Region. In men's clothing, for instance, the first outside gainers were the competing urban centers of Philadelphia and Baltimore; but in the 1930's relative gains were registered by smaller communities of Pennsylvania, Maryland, and the Midwest. In children's outerwear and women's undergarments, after the earlier migration into various counties of the Region, a more recent expansion of employment took place in the low wage Southeast.

This pattern of locational shifts is not unique to the apparel field. The very same process of "peeling off" can be observed in other industries.

A good example is provided by another major industrial group in the New York Metropolitan Region—printing and publishing. Printers' wages have long been higher in New York City than anywhere else in the country except Chicago. On the other hand, the New York area has offered important advantages to publishers. Communication among publishers, authors, and artists has been fast and easy, and specialized firms have provided unique services in art work, translations, book warehousing, and other needs. Moreover, financial offices and establishments providing business services, as we pointed out earlier, have required immediate access to and quick service from the commercial printers. New York City and the Region as a whole, therefore, have retained their position as the major center of publishing and printing.

But drastic changes in the speed of delivery and communication—fast truck delivery, the teletype, stereotype mats, and other devices—have made possible the removal of certain kinds of production to lower cost areas.[5] The publishing activities and the specialized printing for financial, advertising, and legal institutions have stayed and expanded in the Region. But the situation has been different for certain other kinds of printed products. The production of staple items, such as sales forms, moved to lower wage areas on the Atlantic seaboard, in New England, and in parts of the middle South. Much of the printing and binding of books shifted to similar locations.[6]

Thus, despite the great differences between apparel and printing, the locational shifts in the two industries have had important common features. In both cases the affected segments of the industries have been the lines which benefit least from the economic environment of the Region and which are most exposed to the competitive pressures of low wage areas. Very similar shifts in wage-oriented activities have taken place in other industries of the New York Metropolitan Region—in footwear, textiles, electronics. Here, too, the pull of low wage areas has been strongest for the segments which are least subject to rapid changes in products and which have the least need for skilled labor.

IMPACT ON THE REGION'S EMPLOYMENT

What effect have these locational changes had on the number of jobs in the New York Metropolitan Region and on their distribution within the area? A detailed analysis of long-run employment trends in the Region is beyond the scope of this volume. Another volume in this series deals with the problem in depth and detail.* From the wealth of material presented in that study, we can extract some key results and gain an idea of the magnitude of the labor-market influence.

By now, we know enough about wage and skill influences to concentrate our attention upon the manufacturing sector. And, within the manufacturing sector, our attention must be centered upon the group whose markets are more than merely local—our so-called national-market group. Within this group, it appears, employment has grown much more slowly in the Region than it has grown for the same industries in the nation. The comparison appears in Table 31.[7]

How much of this decline was due to wage and skill factors? Everything that we have learned so far counsels caution in framing our answer. This lag in the employment growth of the Region's national-market industries could have been due in part to many factors other than labor. A long-run trend in manufacturing employment is a many-sided phenomenon, reflecting the influence of many forces, often factors in complex combination. We have already seen, for instance, that transport changes facilitated the relocation of even those kinds of manufacturing whose locational motivation was the cost of labor.

Yet, we can isolate the influence of labor in some measure by break-

* The study was conducted by Robert M. Lichtenberg and will constitute part of his book, *One-Tenth of a Nation*. The technical problems involved in the analysis of the employment trends are discussed by Lichtenberg.

Table 31 Percentage Employment Growth in National-Market Industries, New York Metropolitan Region and United States, 1929–1954

Period	Region	U.S.
1929–1939	+ 3.2	+ 6.9
1939–1947	+47.0	+50.0
1947–1954	+ 7.7	+13.9

Note: Industries included in the U. S. figures are limited to those which are present in the Region. In the calculation of the employment growth rate of the U. S., each industry was given the relative weight that it had in the Region's employment.

Source: Robert M. Lichtenberg of the New York Metropolitan Region Study on basis of U. S. *Census of Manufactures* for the various years.

ing down our national-market industries into the groups presented at the early stages of this book—in Table 3 of Chapter 1. The breakdown suggests that transport considerations cannot be invoked to explain much of the sluggishness in the employment growth of the Region's industries, particularly the sluggishness of the postwar years. Industries whose location is primarily determined by a desire to minimize transport costs have shown a relatively good rate of employment growth in the Region, a rate somewhat higher than that in the nation as a whole. Behind this picture of strength in the Region's transport-oriented industries lies a complex story; among other things, it includes the fact that industries once concentrated in the Midwest have been regionalizing their plants in some cases in response to changes in the level and structure of transport rates.*

Similarly, the growth lag of employment in the Region's national-market industries does not appear to be in the main a consequence of the desire to become more centrally located with respect to the national market as populations shifted westward. In general, the Region "exports" goods which have a high value in relation to transport costs; and, if producers of such goods have to ship from a place

* This subject is discussed in detail by Benjamin Chinitz in his volume on freight transportation in this series.

which is off center, they do not suffer much from that circumstance. Indeed, the rise of air freight permits quick shipments of high-value goods to distant markets without imposing significant cost handicaps on the Region's producers.

Aside from transportation, what are some of the other nonlabor factors that help to explain the retarded growth of the Region's industries? One is the rapid population growth in some western urban areas, creating new external economies and bringing in skilled labor and entrepreneurial talent; new plants established in such areas compete in national markets with those of the Region. Other factors include lower rents outside the Region and tax exemptions in Puerto Rico, which have entered into managerial decisions even in the primarily wage-oriented shifts in the garment trades. Though it is impossible to isolate the effects of any one force, the labor market is clearly a major factor contributing to the relatively poor employment performance of the New York industries. Indeed, as we examine the various influences mentioned above, they seem to be less important than the locational impact of the high wage environment in the Region, an environment which has caused a continuous breaking away of segments of manufacturing most vulnerable to competitive pressures from areas where labor costs are lower.

Certainly this factor has been the predominant one in the key sector of industries competing in national markets—the consumer-goods industries which are in the Region primarily because of external economies. These industries, of course, contain standardized lines which are acutely sensitive to wage differentials. As Table 32 shows, the employment growth of these industries in the Region has been retarded; and this has been due to the relatively poor performance of the apparel sector, which dominates the Region's "mix" of consumer goods and which, as we saw, has been continuously subjected to competitive pressures from low wage locations.

The data presented in Table 32 show another significant fact which has a bearing on the locational influence of the Region's labor market. The Region's industries in this group performed much better in relation to their competitors in some periods than in others. The com-

Table 32 Percentage Employment Growth in Selected National-Market Industries Producing Consumer Goods, New York Metropolitan Region and United States, 1929–1954

Period	Region	U. S.
1929–1939	+24.5	+28.4
1939–1947	+29.6	+29.9
1947–1954	+ 4.3	+ 9.4

Notes: Industries included in the U. S. figures are limited to those which are present in the Region. In the calculation of the employment growth rate of the U. S., each industry was given the relative weight that it had in the Region's employment.

Source: Estimates by Robert M. Lichtenberg of the New York Metropolitan Region Study.

petitive weaknesses in the standardized segments of the Region's industries came to the fore during the late 1920's and the 1930's. But the wartime period temporarily reduced competitive pressures from low wage areas.

To be sure, we know from other sources that the Region's *total* employment grew more slowly than elsewhere during the war, since industries producing war materiel were heavily concentrated in other areas. But in the garment and other consumer industries—those included in the table—the New York producers were favored over those in other areas, for it was difficult in wartime to establish new facilities outside; and it was difficult for newcomers in the industry to obtain raw materials.

In the postwar years, however, the competition of low wage areas again began to play an important role in influencing employment trends in the New York Metropolitan Region. The Region's shares of national employment in several industries which have wage-oriented segments—in apparel, book printing, electronics—resumed or accelerated their decline. This is further illustrated in Table 33, which presents postwar employment changes in selected industries.

All the industries in Table 33 contain segments whose location is largely determined by labor-market considerations. The Census classifications, however, are too crude to isolate these segments. As a

Table 33 Ratio of New York Area [a] Employment to National Employment, Selected Industries, 1947 and 1954

(per cent)

	1947	1954
Textiles		
Textile dyeing, finishing	24.9	20.0
Men's apparel		
Men's and boys' suits, coats	26.3	21.8
Dress shirts, nightwear	11.2	8.7
Separate trousers	14.7	9.4
Women's apparel		
Blouses, waists	50.9	40.2
Dresses, unit-priced	62.0	57.1
Coats, suits, and skirts [b]	62.0	55.8
Women's, children's underwear	42.6	32.1
Women's outerwear	34.9	30.6
Children's apparel		
Children's dresses	39.8	38.2
Children's coats and other outerwear [c]	55.4	47.3
Printing and publishing		
Books: publishing and printing	53.1	43.4
Book printing	31.6	24.8
Greeting cards	26.4	25.8
Blank book making	28.7	20.3
Electronics		
Electronic tubes	34.7	16.2

[a] New York area in this table means the 17-county Standard Metropolitan Area which contains more than 90 per cent of the employment of the 22-county New York Metropolitan Region.

[b] In 1947, "skirts" constituted a separate industrial category. By using the breakdown of "skirt" and "coat and suit" production given in the *1954 Census of Manufactures* for manufacturers and jobbers, we can estimate the change in the shares of the New York area for both types of product. These estimates show that in "skirts" the New York share declined from 66.6 per cent in 1947 to 55.6 per cent in 1954; and in "coats and suits" from 61.4 to 55.6 per cent.

[c] Here it was necessary to combine two industries—"children's coats" and "children's outerwear, not elsewhere classified"—because the Census Bureau included "children's skirts" in the first industry in 1947 and in the other in 1954.

Source: U. S. *Census of Manufactures* for 1947 and 1954.

result, we cannot show statistically what we learned in the process of our interviews—that the declines in employment shares have been caused by migration of the least expensive and most standardized products within the individual industries. But in the important industry of women's and misses' dresses there is such evidence, drawn from union sources. This evidence indicates that between 1946 and 1956, by far the largest decline in New York City's share of the nation's dress production payroll was in the lowest price lines. In contrast, the highest price lines in New York City maintained an almost constant share of the national payroll.[8]

The relative "normalcy" of the postwar years has seen also the continuation of another influence of labor-market conditions: the push of garment industries toward location in the counties of the Region outside New York City. As shown in Appendix C, the share of those counties in the Region's garment employment has increased in most industries. We saw earlier that there are important reasons apart from labor for the continuous outward movement of manufacturing facilities within the Region. Lower rents, space for larger facilities, and a relative lack of congestion undoubtedly have played a role in inducing garment establishments to locate outside New York City. But one of the inducements appears to have been the still-existing wage differences and the availability of female labor.

THE PRESENT WAGE-ORIENTED SECTOR

For all the movement of wage-oriented activities to other areas, the New York Metropolitan Region, as we have seen, had some 60,000 to 80,000 jobs in this category in the mid-1950's. Since the wage-oriented establishments of the Region are being exposed to competition from a larger and larger number of outside firms which enjoy substantially lower wage costs, only a drastic change in the relative wage levels of the Region could keep those establishments from declining, expiring, or leaving the area.

But, in examining the postwar wage trends among the Region's industries from 1947 to 1955, we detected no such drastic change. As we view the evidence accumulated in the preceding chapters, there appear scarcely any reasons to believe that the firms under wage pressure—in the garment complex and other industries—will be able to overcome the competitive disadvantage of their present location in the Region. General economic conditions in the 1960's will probably resemble those of the late 1940's and the 1950's. If there is any new long-run trend, it is likely to be toward a less fully employed economy, or at least toward an economy with less pressure of demand upon the nation's resources. In any case, we do not anticipate a drastic wave of labor migration to the major urban areas, a wave so large as to exhaust what is still a relatively ample supply of labor in the rural areas and smaller communities of the country.

Locational shifts of industry to the less industrialized sections of the country will undoubtedly continue to foster the existing trend toward greater uniformity of wages throughout the country. However, as the postwar period suggests, this kind of shift can go on for a long time before it improves the position of wage-oriented producers in the Region. And, similarly, unless there is a drastic change in the public attitude toward minimum wages, it is not reasonable to anticipate that the Fair Labor Standards Act or similar legislation will provide a solution to the troubles of those producers.

Neither can we expect that collective bargaining will significantly narrow interregional wage differences. True, the less industrialized areas of the country will probably experience a relatively greater growth of unionism than the well organized major urban centers. But the unions in highly competitive industries such as the garment trades cannot be counted upon to reduce interregional wage differences very much and thus to improve significantly the competitive position of the Region's producers.

And, finally, this competitive position will find no enhancement in the interrelated movements of wages within the Region, for we cannot reasonably expect that the garment industries in the Region will lag further behind the rest of the Region's economy in the rate of their wage advances. Only a part of the garment complex falls in what we call the wage-oriented category. As garment firms experience intolerable difficulties in attracting new labor, many of them will be able and willing to offer wage increases. Moreover, if garment wages were to persist in rising more slowly than others in the Region, union leaders would encounter internal political problems which already seem to manifest themselves in accusations that the interests of the Puerto Rican workers are being neglected by the garment unions. It is a reasonable expectation, therefore, that in the future the garment and related industries will follow more closely the general trend of wages in the Region. And, as this takes place, the wage-oriented producers in those industries will find themselves under still greater competitive pressure from low wage areas, a pressure which they are not likely to withstand.

Everything in our discussion, therefore, points toward one conclusion. The future will witness a locational shift in what is now the wage-oriented sector of the New York Metropolitan Region. Some of the firms now located in the Region will simply liquidate; their share of the market will be taken up by more suitably located establishments. Other firms may actually move to New England or Pennsylvania. Whatever form the locational shift takes, it will involve the disappearance of 60,000 to 80,000 jobs from the local scene.

COUNTERVAILING FORCES

Though the "peeling off" of the Region's wage-oriented segments of manufacturing reflects a weakness in the Region's competitive position, this is only one aspect of the economic development of the area. While shedding its wage-oriented segments, the Region has provided a highly advantageous economic environment for other types of industrial activity. It has also acted as a magnet attracting new firms and new products. Therefore, we have to view the locational influence of the labor market alongside that of other forces which have been shaping the industrial make-up of the Region.

Even in manufacturing—which is the only segment of the Region's economy affected by wage-oriented locational shifts—the Region has managed to retain a roughly constant share of the nation's employment over the last thirty years. A slight decline in that share did take place prior to 1929. But since then the Region has continued to hold on to about 12 per cent of the nation's manufacturing employment. This, we must emphasize, is a remarkable record, quite different from that of other metropolitan areas in the Northeast, all of which have experienced a steady decline in their shares of national employment in manufacturing.

How can we explain this unusual stability of the Region's share in the face of the westward shifting of the nation's population? Furthermore, how can we reconcile it with our previous conclusion that locational shifts for labor reasons had caused national-market industries to grow more slowly in the Region than in the nation?

As a statistical phenomenon, the stability of the Region's share in manufacturing employment is explained chiefly in terms of the industrial composition, or *mix,* of its manufacturing sector.[9] The Region has continuously had a high concentration of industries whose employment in the nation as a whole has been growing relatively fast. These industries as a group have not grown as rapidly in the Region as they have in the nation; and thus in many individual industries, the Region's share of employment has been declining. But manufacturing in the United States also contains many industries whose rate of growth has been very slow or whose total employment has been going down. From the point of view of employment growth, the nation's mix of manufacturing is less favorable than that of the New York Metropolitan Region.

This fact enters importantly into any comparison between employment growth of *all* manufacturing in the Region and that of all manufacturing in the nation. The Region has retained its share of total manufacturing employment because the favorable composition of its manufacturing activity has offset the effects of declines in its share of fast-growing industries.

Though this explains the statistical results, it does not provide a full answer to our problem. The real question is why the Region has continually attracted industries whose national rate of employment growth is higher than that of manufacturing as a whole; why, indeed, the Region has been so different in this respect from other metropolitan areas of the Northeast.

Here we must recall our early description of the locational advantages of the Region—the highly developed external economies, the ease of communication with multitudes of suppliers and buyers, the pool of labor possessing varied skills, and the presence of productive facilities which can be contracted for and which reduce the investment requirements for newly established firms. These characteristics provide the underlying explanation of the statistical phenomenon of stability in the share of national employment in manufacturing.

As a result of these characteristics, the Region has long provided a highly suitable environment for industries which manufacture changing products, products which are neither standardized nor can be produced in a standardized and routine manner. Much of the Region's manufacturing has indeed specialized in goods which are subject to short-run modifications in design or technology.

Now, as long as technology or product design are not stabilized, and as long as demand for the output continues to expand, this type of industry is likely to experience a relatively fast growth of employment. Without the introduction of highly mechanized and standardized processes operating on long runs of particular products, output per man-hour is not likely to increase rapidly, certainly not as rapidly as for manufacturing as a whole. Hence, expansion of output will be accompanied by relatively large increases in employment.

This is, of course, the story of large portions of the apparel field. Such industries as women's dress manufacturing, by the very nature of their product, cannot dispense with rapid changes in design or operate without uncertainty about the success of a particular style. Accordingly, the bulk of the dress industry's output cannot be standardized and produced on a very large scale in a way which would rapidly increase man-hour productivity. As a result, the industry has experienced a relatively fast rate of employment growth. And the very same factors which explain this employment growth keep a high concentration of dress producers in the New York Metropolitan Region—in an environment which so well facilitates adaptability of individual firms to changing fashions and designs.

If changes in technology or demand went always in one direction, if the constant tendency of the economy were toward more standardized goods and routinized methods of production, the Region's manufacturing employment would not have withstood so well the shifts of wage-oriented firms. The fact is that industries have also undergone changes which made their products subject to modifications or which compelled the firms to seek continual and quick contacts with customers and suppliers.

Earlier we mentioned the knit outerwear industry, which became fashion-conscious and began producing stylish sweaters and suits whose designs are constantly modified. Analogous changes have taken place in various types of apparel accessories which have also become subject to rapid changes in fashion and design. Most importantly, the growth of business activities—advertising agencies, central offices, and others—has affected the products of the printing and publishing industries. While some segments of printing output were being standardized, other segments have been developing toward more rapid service and higher variability of product for these new customers in the Region.

All these changes have run counter to the tendency toward standardization of products and production methods. But the Region has not been merely a passive beneficiary of the changes which mitigate the tendency toward standardization. The Region's economic environment—the combination of external economies and relatively high wages—has itself provided a stimulus toward development of differentiated and variable products. As firms producing more standardized types of apparel or toys begin to feel the impact of outside competition, they are under pressure to modify their product in order to protect themselves, temporarily at least, from the competitive pressures based on lower labor costs elsewhere. And as these innovations find public acceptance, the trend to standardization in some product lines is accompanied by an increasing emphasis on style or changing design in other lines.

What is true of location in established industries like dresses or toys applies with an even greater force to completely new types of economic activity, to industries which are still experimenting with their products and still undergoing rapid changes in technology. Students of the New York Metropolitan Region observed long ago that the area offers an especially attractive location "for new enterprises during the early formative and experimental stages." [10] And, indeed, the Region has fulfilled the role of nursery for a wide variety of industries, offering them advantages of external economies—including its large pool of skilled craftsmen—and providing opportunities for personal contacts with patent experts, legal advisers, and financiers interested in new products.

Many new firms, it is true, have used the Region as a sort of experiment station and have moved away as soon as output and methods of production have become settled and standardized. But the Region's nursery benefits have enabled it to attract other new and fast-growing activities to take the places of the ones that have left. And this process has contributed to the fact that the Region's manufacturing has always been weighted heavily with industries experiencing a rapid rise in employment.

The stability of the Region's share of national manufacturing employment, therefore, is not a fortuitous phenomenon, but is rooted in the basic characteristics of the Region's economy—characteristics that have provided countervailing forces to the competitive pressures which originate in low wage areas and which lead to locational shifts in selected segments of the Region's manufacturing.

PROSPECTS FOR A CHANGING METROPOLIS

As we view the course of economic development in the New York Metropolitan Region, two basic features clearly stand out. First, as a consequence of its special combination of locational advantages, the Region has experienced growth of its total manufacturing employment which is unique among the metropolitan areas of the Northeast. And, second, this growth has been accompanied by a continual change in the industrial make-up of the area, a change in which the Region's labor-market conditions have played an important role. On the one hand, the Region's pool of skills—as part of the entire complex of external economies—has helped the Region to attract new types of specialized activities. On the other hand, the Region's high wages have been pushing away jobs which could be performed with equal facility and at lower cost elsewhere.

We cannot tell, on the basis of the facts developed in this volume, whether the Region will continue its remarkable performance in manufacturing employment. A great deal depends on such factors as the rise of external economies in other areas, changes in the methods of transportation, and trends in population movements. Only the final synthesis of all the studies in this series can consider these and other factors affecting the future economic growth of the Region. But the present study does provide an important insight into the future. For, as we review all the evidence presented above, one implication emerges clearly.

Regardless of the ultimate course of its economic development in the next two decades, the New York Metropolitan Region will continue to experience an outbound movement of wage-oriented jobs.

The slow narrowing of interregional wage differences in the nation is not likely to come to full fruition for decades. And the rate at which employment grows in the New York Metropolitan Region cannot have much influence on the continuing high wage position of the area. If the Region's job opportunities do not expand as fast as those of other areas, the primary effect is not likely to appear in lower wage levels, but rather in the slowdown of in-migration of Puerto Ricans and Negroes and of other workers from small communities or rural areas. So long as migration does not exhaust the supply of cheap labor in outside communities, and so long as the more complex and specialized jobs are not evenly distributed throughout the country, the Region must inevitably remain a relatively high wage area.

It is thus apparent that the potential displacement from the Region of what are presently its wage-oriented jobs does not represent the end of the locational impact of the labor market. Changes in technology or public tastes will continue affecting what today are still relatively unstandardized types of production in the Region.

Faster trucks and improved networks of highways will further facilitate transportation to and from outlying communities of New England, the Middle Atlantic states, and the Southeast. The expansion of air transport and of such devices as closed circuit television will undoubtedly free new firms from relying on the advantages of the urban environment. And, as these developments change the locational orientation of particular lines, the New York Metropolitan Region will continue to spawn wage-oriented jobs and to lose them to labor markets having lower wage levels.

It is not our task either to set goals for public policy or to recommend the ways in which any particular goals should be implemented. But even so, the preceding discussion does have implications for those who will have a hand in future decisions affecting the Region.

One implication is that public policies can have only a limited impact—if any at all—on the Region's position as a high wage area. It is true that certain steps can have the effect of increasing the local supply of labor for standardized lines of garment-making, electronics, or even printing. Thus, measures to induce greater migration of Puerto Ricans or Negroes into the Region—measures such as the provision of low-income housing and the improvement of job information programs for prospective migrants—can furnish the Region's producers with a larger pool of relatively cheap labor than they could otherwise have. Yet, clearly, such measures cannot overcome the effect of the forces which make the Region a relatively high wage area, and they will not significantly enhance the ability of the Region to compete with other areas for the location of wage-oriented activities.

Another implication—the other side of the coin—is that, if the Region is to retain a high rate of employment growth, it can do this only through the unique locational advantages that it offers to the complex, the variable, and the highly specialized types of economic pursuits. Policies directed toward the enhancement of these advantages have a stronger chance of making themselves felt in the economic development of the Region. One such measure in the field of labor is the institution or expansion of training programs for skilled workers and technicians. But there are other measures as well, falling outside the scope of this book, such as improvements in the transportation of goods and people within the Region—improvements which would spread the benefits of external economies to its various parts. All told, such measures can contribute to the Region's continued growth and can move in the direction of offsetting the loss in jobs which will result from the Region's essential character as a high wage area.

Acknowledgment

In doing research connected with this study, I received important help from Miss Mildred Lauder of the New York State Department of Labor, Division of Employment; Dr. Lawrence Kaplan, formerly of the New York Regional Office of the Bureau of Labor Statistics; and my cousin, Martin E. Segal, of Martin E. Segal and Company.

MARTIN SEGAL

Appendix A
Sources and Methods

Like politics, the construction of statistics to measure interregional wage differentials may be said to be the art of the possible. Of the large amount of available wage data, whether compiled by the U. S. Bureau of Labor Statistics, by state agencies, by the U. S. Bureau of the Census, or by private research organizations, hardly any of the statistics are well suited for interregional wage comparisons. The problem facing us was how to choose those statistics which would come closest to what we are really after—data revealing wage differences attributable to differences in the location of the establishments.

THE BASIC SOURCES

As indicated in Chapter 2, the available information suggests that workers in various sections of the United States do not show any systematic differences in productivity. If this is so, a reliable index of labor-cost differences among different locations could be obtained from wage data, provided certain conditions were satisfied. Though located in different areas, the plants involved would have to be essentially alike in the following characteristics: type of output, competitive position of the firm in the product market, skill composition of the work force, distribution between time and incentive workers in each occupational category of workers, and size of establishment. The interregional wage differences shown by this type of data could then be attributed primarily to a combination of factors reflecting the conditions of the local labor market, such as demand for and supply of labor, the industrial composition of the local economy, and the relative strength of collective bargaining in the area.

The available wage data which approach this ideal most closely are those collected by the U. S. Bureau of Labor Statistics in a series of industry studies published in a series of pamphlets under the general title *Wage Structure.** These studies provide wage data on individual occupations of the industry in various geographical areas. They also provide a great deal of information on supplementary employee benefits and, in some cases, on the extent of collective bargaining in a particular area. By and large these are undoubtedly the most detailed sets of wage statistics produced in this country. However, from the point of view of our study these statistics are still not sufficiently detailed.

One difficulty arises because of the variations in the product mix of plants from one area to another. Even within the narrow industrial categories used in the Census of Manufactures—the so-called "four-digit" categories—there are differences in the type of output produced by different plants. These differences may affect interregional wage comparisons. For one thing, the competitive market structure may vary from one product line to another. This variation is likely to be reflected in the wage policies of individual firms. For another, the actual skills, even though presumed to be constant in any *occupational* classification, may vary widely depending on the nature of the product line of the establishment.

Some of the BLS wage structure studies pertain to four-digit classifications. But others cover broader groupings, composed of more than one four-digit industry. In such cases the problem of variation in the product mix of various locations may be quite significant.

Another limitation of the BLS studies on wage structure is that they generally do not classify occupational earnings in a particular community by size of the plants. Since the various areas do not have

* A good recent example is *Wage Structure, Women's and Misses' Coats and Suits* (BLS Report No. 122), February 1957.

the same plant size distribution, this factor also influences inter-area wage comparisons.

Finally, the BLS studies on wage structure do not cover the entire area of the New York Metropolitan Region. In some of the important industries they include the ten most industrialized counties of the Region—the five boroughs of New York City and the five New Jersey counties containing and surrounding Newark, Jersey City, and Paterson. (These counties are Essex, Hudson, Union, Passaic, and Bergen.) In other cases, however, the coverage is limited to New York City and the three counties of the Newark–Jersey City area (that is, Essex, Hudson, and Union). In spite of these limitations, the wage data in these BLS studies are still superior, from our point of view, to other available wage data, and we used them as extensively as possible. Specifically, we utilized all the wage structure studies conducted in 1955 and later years which covered New York City and the Newark–Jersey City area. Fortunately, these recent studies included the two important women's apparel industries: women's and misses' dresses and women's coats and suits. We also used some earlier BLS studies as a general check on the wage data obtained from other sources, and as information supplementing the patterns of wage differences emerging from our comparisons.

For a large portion of our inter-area wage comparisons, we had to rely on statistics of average hourly earnings. The limitations of average hourly earnings as a measure of the price of labor are well known. Plants in various locations differ with respect to amount of overtime and holiday work, proportion of incentive workers, skill composition of the work force, and so on. The skill composition of the work force is undoubtedly the most important source of differences in average hourly earnings not related to differences in the price of labor. We tried to limit the effect of this factor by comparing average hourly earnings only for the most narrowly defined industrial groupings—the four-digit classifications used in the Census of Manufactures. The use of these narrow industrial groupings limited to some extent the possibilities of variations in skill composition which may be caused by differences in the product mix of plants in different locations.

The extent to which variations in skill composition affect comparisons of average hourly earnings depends on the nature of the particular industry. The effect is probably smallest in such industries as petroleum refining or beer manufacturing, in which the nature of the equipment restricts variations in the composition of the work force; or in such manufacturing industries as paperboard boxes or paints and varnishes, which use little skilled labor. But we can expect very considerable variation in the skill mix of different shops in some of the apparel industries, since such shops use a great deal of both manual and skilled labor, and since the number of skilled hands in a shop depends on the price line of the product. As pointed out, however, for some of the most important industries in apparel we were able to use the BLS wage structure studies and thus compare earnings of a uniform occupational mix in the Region and other locations. In other industries, such as footwear or men's suits and coats, a check of the older BLS wage structure studies appeared to confirm the essential pattern of wage differences shown by the comparisons of average hourly earnings. Finally, in several cases where the earlier BLS studies showed considerable differences in occupational mix among areas, we had to discard the data on average hourly earnings.

The decision to use only the narrowest industrial classifications in the average hourly earnings comparisons meant, of necessity, a limitation on the number of industries whose interregional wage differences could be analyzed. Most of the average hourly earnings statistics published by various state agencies pertain to broader industrial classifications. The same is true of the U. S. *1954 Census of Manufactures.* We resorted therefore, to special tabulations of average hourly earnings for the narrowest industrial classification, made for the New York Metropolitan Region Study by the U. S. Bureau of Labor Statistics and the New York State Department of Labor. These tabulations were prepared from the data collected by state agencies under the integrated federal-state project which produces the BLS series of hours and earnings for the nation.*

In addition to the wage statistics described above, we used three other types of wage data:

(a) In order to determine the trends in wage differences among the broad sections of the country we used average hourly earnings computed from data on wages and hours in the U.S. *Census of Manufactures* for 1947 and 1954. These data have all the limitations of statistics on average hourly earnings. Once again we used only the narrowest industrial classifications available, attempting thereby to limit the effect of interplant variations in the skill mix of the work force. (See note on page 85.)

(b) In making the comparison of wages in the construction industry, we relied both on the surveys by various trade publications and on the BLS bulletins which give union wage rates annually in all the major urban areas. Except for a few isolated cases, the wage data in both types of source were identical. This suggests that the union-negotiated rates are used by the construction industry throughout the country to compare labor costs in various locations. We also used union wage rates in the local transit industry, to compare differences among cities. The use of union rates in this industry is justified by the fact that the transit workers of every major city are covered by collective bargaining agreements.

(c) Our final major source of data was the BLS community wage surveys, published under the general title *Occupational Wage Survey*.† These surveys cover a particular area rather than an industry. The comparison of office workers' salaries and the comparison of workers' wages in wholesale trade are based on the data derived from this source.

The *Occupational Wage Surveys* are by far the best available

* For a description of the techniques used in collecting these statistics see Bureau of Labor Statistics, *Techniques of Preparing Major BLS Statistical Series* (Bulletin No. 1168, Washington, 1954), Chap. 7.

† See for example, Bureau of Labor Statistics, *Occupational Wage Survey, New York, New York, April 1956* (Bulletin No. 1188–17).

source of salary data. Yet they too have limitations from our point of view. One of these limitations is the fact that the minimum size of establishments covered by the surveys is either 50 or 100 employees, depending on the area. Salaries in smaller establishments are excluded. Another limitation is that the surveys were not conducted at precisely the same time in different areas; in some cases the difference in timing is several months.

COMPUTING EARNINGS INDICES

As we have already indicated, we used wage data derived from the BLS *Wage Structure* series wherever possible. From these studies we obtained hourly earnings of individual occupations in a particular industry in each of the geographical areas covered by the relevant survey. From these earnings, in turn, we computed average industry earnings for each area, and compared them with their counterparts in the Region.

In computing average industry earnings, we used a uniform occupational mix for all areas. For manufacturing industries, the occupational weights used were the numbers of workers in the various occupations in the sample of establishments in the New York Metropolitan Region. For service and office workers, the weights were the number of workers in the various occupations in New York City.* Male and female workers in the same occupation, such as the occupation of "hand pressers" in the women's dress industry, were considered as two separate occupations. The general formula for the earnings comparison in each industry between the Region and other areas is as follows:

$$\frac{\sum_{j=1}^{n} W_a^j E_r^j}{\sum_{j=1}^{n} W_r^j E_r^j}$$

where W_a^j = wage in occupation j in area A; W_r^j = wage in occupation j in the New York Metropolitan Region; E_r^j = numbers

* In each case the weights were derived from the most recent wage survey.

of workers in occupation j in the New York Metropolitan Region in the most recent sample of establishments surveyed by the Bureau of Labor Statistics. (Usually this means the sample in the New York City–Newark–Jersey City area. In some industries the sample includes also Paterson; in services, the weights are derived from the sample in New York City.)

In constructing the indices of average earnings from individual occupational earnings, we encountered the problem of the differences in the skill composition of the industry's work force in various areas. In any industry the skill composition of the work force may vary from one area to another for two reasons. For one thing, the variation may be a result of differences in the product mix of the differently located establishments. In such cases, the industry groupings covered by the survey are too broad to assure a uniformity of the skill mix in the plants classified in the same industry.

In addition, the structure of occupational wage differences may vary among the different geographical areas. For example, if in area *A* the ratio of skilled wage rates to semiskilled wage rates is higher than the equivalent ratio in community *B*, then, other things being equal, the employers in *A* are likely to use relatively more semiskilled and less skilled labor than their counterparts in *B*.

The standardization of occupational mix for the purpose of interarea comparison limits the effect of the first factor, that is, the effect of the difference in the product mix among areas. But it does not solve the second problem, that of variations resulting from substitution of less costly grades of labor for more expensive grades.

In most industries the use of the occupational mix of the New York Metropolitan Region as weights did not raise any problem. The differences in occupational mix among areas were small and appeared to reflect differences in the product mix. But the problem is more important in the women's and misses' dress industry and to some extent also in women's coats and suits.

In the dress industry the basic difference between the occupational mix of the Region and that of other areas is in the relative numerical importance of sewing machine operators under the "tailor system" (hand) and sewing machine operators under the "section system." In the Region the tailor-system operators are by far the most important occupational group in numerical terms; but in most other areas, section-system operators are considerably more numerous. One reason is that the Region produces a larger proportion of more expensive dresses than other areas. But this appears to be only a partial explanation.

As pointed out in Chapter 3, most of the operators in the lowest price lines in New York City are tailor-system operators. The section-system operators are employed largely in medium or higher price lines where they can earn about the same wages as the tailor-system operators in the lowest price lines. Apparently in order to induce New York workers to work on a section-system basis, employers must pay relatively high wages. Such wages are more feasible in the more expensive price lines in which the negotiated piece rates are higher. In effect, then, section-system operators in the Region are paid higher wages relative to tailor-system operators than is the case in most other areas. This is indicated by Table A–1, which expresses the earnings of both types of sewing machine operators in selected locations as a percentage of the respective earnings in the

Table A–1 Earnings of Female Sewing Machine Operators, Tailor System and Section System, in Women's and Misses' Dress Industry, 1955

(selected areas [a] as percentage of New York–Newark–Jersey City–Paterson area)

Occupation	Boston	Chicago	Los Angeles	Philadelphia	St. Louis	Dallas
Tailor-system operators ...	83.57	94.18	81.64	97.10	71.98	57.97
Section-system operators ...	74.60	72.49	87.83	73.54	65.08	60.32

[a] These are Standard Metropolitan Areas, except that Chicago means Cook County only; and Philadelphia means Delaware and Philadelphia Counties, both in Pennsylvania, and Camden County, New Jersey.

Source: U. S. Bureau of Labor Statistics, *Women's and Misses Dresses, 1955,* Forms OWR–24 for individual areas.

Region. Generally the earnings differential between the Region and other areas is greater for the section-system operators than for tailor-system operators. A notable exception is Los Angeles, but in this area the bulk of workers, like those in the New York Metropolitan Region, work on a tailor-system basis.

Given the data presented in Table A–1, we can see that, insofar as the difference in the skill mix of the work force between, say, Philadelphia and the New York Metropolitan Region is a result of the difference in relative wages of the two types of operators, the wage comparison based on the Region's occupational mix understates the Region's wage position in relation to Philadelphia. The same may be said of the comparison with Chicago or St. Louis, and to a lesser degree with Boston.

In women's coats and suits, the New York Metropolitan Region is characterized by a predominance of men in the occupation of sewing machine operators working on the tailor system; in some other areas, such as San Francisco and Los Angeles, the proportion of men in this occupation is much smaller. In comparison with other areas, the differential between male and female wages in the Region is small. In other words, it is relatively easier to recruit men than women for this occupation in the Region, as compared with other areas. In fact, in some areas the wages of male sewing machine operators in this industry are higher than in New York.

The use of a standardized occupational mix based on the Region's work force results again in some understatement of the relative wage position of New York in women's coats and suits. But here the effect is not as large as in the dress industry. And we must also bear in mind that the difference in the sex composition of the work force may be partly the result of differences in the product mix, with men employed more extensively in the production of more expensive coats and suits. Insofar as this factor is important, our standardization procedure is quite justified.

The significance of the difficulties discussed above should not be exaggerated. The differences in the relative position of the New York Metropolitan Region which would result from some other method of computing average earnings for the areas would be quite small, and no basic change in the pattern of interregional wage differentials would occur. Almost identical results, for instance, would be obtained if the so-called modified Fisher index formula were used in our computations.

One last point: each comparison between the New York Metropolitan Region and another area is based on an occupational mix which is the same for the Region and the other area. But there are some variations among the occupational mixes which were used for comparing the Region with different areas. For some areas certain occupational wage data were not available; this was usually the case in situations in which a particular occupational group was numerically very small in a given location. In modifying the occupational mix for comparisons from one area to another, we reduced the general accuracy of our over-all inter-area comparisons. But the gain was a more accurate comparison between the Region itself and each alternate area.

✓ Estimates of supplementary employee benefits

Our statistical data on supplementary employee remuneration (fringe benefits) are drawn from three basic sources: from the BLS *Wage Structure* studies for most industries; from the BLS *Occupational Wage Surveys* for office workers and wholesale trade; and from industry and trade magazines, supplemented by special inquiries, for the building trades. We believe that the data reproduced in the study help to form an impression of the relative position of the New York Metropolitan Region in the field of supplementary employee remuneration. Nevertheless, there are considerable differences in the accuracy of the information supplied by our sources.

The most complete types of data pertain to industries in which employers contribute certain amounts—usually a percentage of total payrolls or hourly earnings—to a general fund, usually administered jointly by the employers and the union. In these industries, unions bargain for monetary contributions to a welfare or pension fund rather than some specified standard of benefit. Typically the industries are characterized by the presence of many small firms, intermittent employment, and high mobility of workers from firm to firm—workers who are attached to an industry or trade rather than an establishment. The building trades are, of course, a classic example, but similar arrangements are also negotiated in a variety of other industries, such as the garment industries, laundries, and bakeries.

Our data on the garment industries and the building trades—reflecting the employer contributions to these funds—may be considered as fairly accurate. The main limitation of these data is that they throw little light on the levels of benefit payments in the nonunion sectors of the industry in each area. But, as pointed out in the text, the data on nonunion establishments in the garment trades indicate that the benefits generally are considerably lower there than in union plants.

For other industries our data are subject to many limitations. Our information on the percentage of workers covered by various benefit programs in different areas does not indicate, of course, the degree of liberality of the specific types of programs, such as retirement plans.

Even our data on the paid holidays and vacations, expressed as a percentage of time worked, provide only a rough indication of these costs borne by employers in various areas. At best, our data pertain to the average practices with respect to paid holidays and vacations. To estimate actual costs, one would need a great deal of additional information. For example, two establishments which grant the same number of paid holidays to their employees may incur different expenses, depending not only on their wage levels but also on such factors as eligibility requirements, absenteeism during the week on which the holiday falls, and fluctuations in employment. The costs of vacations depend not only on the period granted for a given length of service and on the plant wage levels, but also on such factors as the rate of labor turnover and the length-of-service distribution of the plant work force. The possible influence of these factors, though perhaps not of paramount importance, will be borne in mind by a careful student of the data.

Field interviews

Supplementing other sources of information, we conducted 68 interviews with businessmen and union leaders in the New York Metropolitan Region. In addition, we drew liberally on the field work and information gathered by various colleagues on the staff of the New York Metropolitan Region Study.

Our interviews did not follow a rigid pattern. In general, however, we concentrated on the procedures used in choosing new locations of productive facilities; on management practices with respect to the training and hiring of employees; on the geographical extent of the markets in which firms sold their products; and on the location of producers competing with New York firms. We also sought information on the nature of collective bargaining in the Region—the extent of contracts negotiated by various labor and employer organizations, the structure of the local unions and employer groups, and the forms of wage increases negotiated in the past. Most of our interviews generated specific factual information rather than opinions. With respect to some issues, however, such as that of interregional comparisons of labor productivity, the results of the interviews inevitably reflect certain value judgments of the interviewees.

Appendix B

Wage Trends inside the Region

This appendix consists of two tables. Table B–1 shows the 1947–1955 percentage wage increases in 44 industries in the New York Metropolitan Region. Part of this table—those industries employing substantial numbers of Puerto Ricans and Negroes—is used as Table 29 in Chapter 5. The other table in this appendix, Table B–2, compares wages in New York City with those in the rest of the Region in 1947 and again in 1955.

Table B–1 Percentage Wage Increases in Selected Services and Manufacturing Industries in New York Metropolitan Region, 1947–1955

I. Garment and related industries	
Median increase	17.8
Corsets, allied garments	45.7
Knit outerwear	39.3
Men's dress shirts, nightwear	35.4
Dyeing, finishing textiles	33.5
Women's underwear, nightwear	28.2
Men's and boys' suits, coats	23.9
Blouses and waists	23.8
Footwear	18.2
Costume jewelry	17.3
Fur goods	16.2
Children's dresses	14.8
Handbags and purses	12.9

Millinery	12.6
Children's coats	11.9
Women's and misses' dresses	8.6
Women's coats, suits, and skirts [a]	7.4

II. Construction and services [a]

Median increase	49.6
Office building services [b]	82.3
Local transit [c]	60.4
Hotels [b]	58.6
Truckdrivers [d]	51.5
Building trades [c]	48.3
Office workers [e]	48.0
Restaurants	46.2
Power laundries [b]	30.0

III. Local-market industries

Median increase	52.4
Malt liquors	77.1
Tin cans and other tinware	62.8
Paints and varnishes	57.0
Ship building and repairing	55.6
Paperboard boxes	54.3
Public utilities	52.4
Bread and bakery products	51.5
Commercial printing	49.7
Metal stampings	46.3
Machine tool accessories [b, f]	39.6
Lighting fixtures	38.2

IV. National-market industries except garment trades

Median increase	47.7
Petroleum refining	58.5
Machinery (nonelectrical) [b, f]	49.6
Toilet preparations	49.5
Plastic materials	48.3
Pharmaceutical products	47.7
Scientific instruments	46.7

Radios and related products	44.9
Motor vehicles, parts	40.4
Confectionery	37.6

Notes: Except as noted below, all percentages are computed from average hourly earnings for the 22 counties of the New York Metropolitan Region.

[a] New York City only.

[b] Computed from hourly earnings of selected occupations.

[c] Computed from union hourly rates. For building trades, we used the weights derived from Boeckh Index Tables for Apartments, Hotels and Office Buildings. For local transit, rates for one-man cars were used.

[d] Average hourly earnings of union drivers.

[e] Weekly salaries were used.

[f] New York City–Newark–Jersey City area.

Sources: Special tabulations of the U.S. Bureau of Labor Statistics and New York State Department of Labor; New York State Department of Labor, *Restaurant Industry,* Publications No. B–5 and B–93; BLS, *Union Wages and Hours* (Bulletins No. 928, 930, 933, 1193, 1195, and 1205); BLS, *Hotels* (1947 and 1955), Forms OWR–24 for New York City; BLS, *Office Building Service* (1947 and 1955), Forms OWR–24 for New York City; BLS, *Power Laundries,* (1947 and 1956), Forms OWR–24 for New York City; BLS, *Machinery Industries* (1947 and 1956), Forms OWR–24 for New York City and Newark–Jersey City; BLS, *Occupational Wage Survey, New York, New York, April 1956* (Bulletin No. 1188–17); BLS, *Office Workers, Salaries, Hours of Work, Supplementary Benefits, New York, New York, January, 1948;* also special information supplied by five major public utilities in the New York Metropolitan Region.

Table B–2 Wages in New York Metropolitan Region outside New York City, Expressed as Percentage of Wages in New York City, Selected Industries, 1947 and 1955

	1947	1955
Garment and related industries		
Children's dresses	82.9	92.7
Women's and misses' dresses [a]	82.3	93.0
Women's underwear and nightwear	81.1	91.2
Blouses and waists	83.0	89.0
Women's coats and suits [b]	84.7	86.7
Corsets and allied garments	90.2	97.4
Knit outerwear	87.3	89.3
Handbags and purses	66.7	82.2
Men's dress shirts and nightwear	90.5	90.8
Other industries		
Building trades [c]	104.8	106.2
Truckdrivers [d]	98.0	101.8
Power laundries [e]	91.2	92.3
Local transit [f]	107.9	101.9
Bread and bakery products	94.0	97.5
Confectionery	107.0	106.6
Malt liquors	88.2	98.2
Paperboard boxes	100.9	105.7
Commercial printing	94.9	99.2
Pharmaceutical preparations	100.8	112.3
Paints and varnishes	105.6	109.5
Toilet preparations	108.1	108.9
Tin cans and other tinware	107.3	116.3
Metal stampings	112.1	100.0
Lighting fixtures	104.1	117.1
Radios and related products	102.6	94.9
Ship building and repairing	101.3	98.3
Machinery (nonelectrical) [g]	99.3	100.5
Machine tool accessories [g]	97.3	101.2

Notes: Except as indicated below, the percentages are derived from average hourly earnings data for New York City and the rest of the Region.

[a] Computed from hourly earnings of selected occupations. Comparison is

between New York City and Newark–Jersey City–Paterson area. Weights based on New York City's occupational mix.

[b] Computed from hourly earnings of selected occupations. Comparison is between New York City and Newark–Jersey City–Paterson area for 1946 and 1957. Weights based on New York City's occupational mix.

[c] Derived from union rates. Weights derived from Boeckh Index Tables for Apartments, Hotels, and Office Buildings. Comparison is between New York City and Newark.

[d] Average hourly earnings of unionized truckdrivers. Comparison is between New York City and Newark.

[e] Computed from hourly earnings of selected occupations. Comparison is between New York City and Newark–Jersey City area. Weights based on New York City's occupational mix.

[f] Union hourly rates for one-man cars were used. Comparison is between New York City and Newark.

[g] Computed from hourly earnings of selected occupations. Comparison is between New York City and Newark–Jersey City area. Weights based on New York City's occupational mix.

Sources: Special tabulations of U. S. Bureau of Labor Statistics and New York State Department of Labor; BLS, *Union Wages and Hours* (Bulletins No. 928, 930, 933, 1193, 1195 and 1205); BLS, Power Laundries (1947 and 1955), Forms OWR–24; BLS, *Machinery Industries* (1947 and 1956), Forms OWR–24; BLS, *Women's and Misses' Dresses* (1947 and 1955), Forms OWR–24; BLS, *Women's Coats and Suits* (1946 and 1947), Forms OWR–24.

Appendix C

Garment Employment in the Region

Table C-1 Changing Distribution of Garment Employment as between New York City and Rest of New York Metropolitan Region, 1947–1956

Selected industries	Employment in Region		New York City's percentage	
	1947	1956	1947	1956
Knit outerwear	15,628	24,775	79.0	76.6
Men's suits and coats	38,797	25,378	82.8	89.9
Men's dress shirts and nightwear	8,589	7,665	54.1	66.4
Blouses and waists	17,214	15,008	83.6	80.7
Women's and misses' dresses	99,765	84,834	84.5	83.1
Women's coats, suits, and skirts	67,721	58,259	80.9	73.1
Women's and children's underwear	26,048	25,674	78.9	80.4
Corsets and allied garments	14,758	16,010	77.1	66.7
Millinery	15,691	13,794	94.5	91.7
Children's dresses	9,312	10,372	74.2	64.1
Children's coats	7,283	8,759	81.3	67.8
Handbags and purses	16,779	16,741	75.1	68.4
Footwear, except rubber	15,131	9,010	92.9	89.7

Source: Data for September 1947 and September 1956 collected by state departments of labor under unemployment insurance programs. Employment for Dutchess, Putnam, and Orange Counties in 1947 estimated from information in the *New York Industrial Directory*.

NOTES

Chapter 1: wages and skills as locational factors

1. Labor-and-space comparisons were based on estimates derived from other volumes in this series. Tax data for manufacturing were taken from the Internal Revenue Service's *Statistics of Income for 1953;* these data were expressed as percentages of gross sales in 1953 and were compared with wages and salaries as percentages of gross value of shipments as derived from the *1954 Census of Manufactures.* Various classification problems limit the accuracy and validity of the comparison, but the data are sufficiently reliable to support the general point in the text.

2. The location near the market may sometimes be a result of institutional arrangements characterizing particular product markets. For example, the producers of paperboard boxes locate near their customers partly because the delivered prices of their basic raw material, paper, are equalized over wide zones. A location which reduces the transport cost of the finished product, therefore, leads to minimum total transport costs.

3. See Richard A. Lester, *Company Wage Policies* (Princeton, N. J., 1948); John T. Dunlop, "The Task of Contemporary Wage Theory," in *New Concepts in Wage Determination,* ed. George W. Taylor and Frank C. Pierson (New York, 1957), p. 136; Lloyd G. Reynolds, *The Structure of Labor Markets* (New York, 1951), pp. 232–234.

4. The comparisons are based on the wages of nonproduction jobs, for which the nomenclature in various industries and plants has more standardized meaning. But they serve well enough to reflect the situation prevailing also in production jobs. For a discussion of reasons for this difference in relative wages among areas see Harry Ober, "Occupational Wage Differentials," in W. Woytinsky and Associates, *Wages and Employment in the United States* (New York: Twentieth Century Fund, 1953), p. 470.

Chapter 2: skill, productivity, and unionization

1. National Manpower Council, *A Policy for Skilled Manpower* (New York, 1954), p. 214.

2. We should bear in mind that the various job titles describing skilled occupations lack preciseness. There are many areas, for example, which appear to have ample supplies of "machinists." Yet this term embraces both highly skilled mechanics employed in the building of equipment and workers performing routine machine operations. Some managements of the Region's firms found out through experience that even when it appears that a particular location such as Richmond, Virginia, has a pool of what is locally consid-

ered as skilled labor, these workers are not as highly trained and experienced as the workers of such areas as New York or Chicago. Similarly, a Bureau of Labor Statistics study suggests that many of the workers who call themselves machinists should be really considered as semiskilled operators. (Compare National Manpower Council, just cited, pp. 46 and 66.)

3. William H. Whyte, Jr., *The Organization Man* (Garden City: Doubleday & Co., 1957), p. 305.

4. These generalizations are further developed and documented in other volumes of this series, based on the work of Benjamin Chinitz and Robert Lichtenberg. See also U. S. Department of Commerce, *Long-Term Regional Trends in Manufacturing Growth: 1899–1955,* Area Trend Series, February 1958.

5. For example, producers of printing equipment tend to be concentrated in New York and Chicago, the dominant centers of the printing and publishing industries.

6. Richard A. Lester, "Effectiveness of Factory Labor: South-North Comparisons," *Journal of Political Economy* (February 1946), pp. 60–75, and the literature cited therein.

7. The South, being one of the less industrialized sections of the country, would presumably show great differences from other sections in workers' attitudes toward industrial employment. Yet the available evidence indicates that the labor force in the South does not display any marked differences in efficiency from that of other areas. See Melvin L. Greenhut, *Plant Location in Theory and in Practice* (Chapel Hill, 1956), pp. 130–131 and the literature cited there.

8. As one study of plant location observed: "A positive guide for probable labor productivity is evasive. Multiplant companies with adequate records and an inclination toward research should have little difficulty in comparing productivity of employees in their various plants. But, unless the prospective employer is already operating in the community under consideration, he is forced into a rather uncritical acceptance of whatever he may be told by other employers in the community." Edward D. Wickersham, *Labor as a Factor in Plant Location in Michigan* (School of Business Administration, University of Michigan, 1957), p. 3.

9. This process has gone a long way in the South and today is of special significance in Puerto Rico, where industrialization is making rapid strides.

10. John T. Dunlop, "The American Industrial Relations System in 1975," in *U. S. Industrial Relations, The Next Twenty Years,* ed. Jack Stieber (Michigan State University Press, 1958), p. 33.

11. Computed from data in Bureau of Labor Statistics, *Directory of National and International Labor Unions in the United States, 1957* (Bulletin No. 1222).

12. See, for instance, B. M. and S. K. Selekman, "Productivity and Collective Bargaining," *Harvard Business Review,* 28:127–144 (March 1950). Indeed, the conclusion of many studies has been that, on balance, union leaders

are likely to facilitate introduction of technological changes, increasing the productivity of plant operations. See the writer's "Factors in Wage Adjustments to Technological Changes," *Industrial and Labor Relations Review* (January 1955), p. 227, and the bibliography cited there.

13. Bargaining through multi-employer groups has significant advantages not only for employers but also for the union. From a purely practical point of view, it would be impossible in many cases for the union to bargain individually with the many employers involved. Moreover, bargaining with employer associations facilitates the introduction of uniform labor standards, limiting competition based on labor-cost differences. For an excellent discussion of multi-employer bargaining in New York City, see Jesse T. Carpenter, *Employers' Associations and Collective Bargaining in New York City* (Ithaca, N. Y., 1950).

14. We should emphasize that the employers' associations are generally constituted in such a way as to reflect the differences of product lines in a given industry. Accordingly, the contract and its administration will reflect the particular conditions, economic and technological, related to the firm's specialized line of product. For example, "the manufacture of headwear is broken down into women's headwear and men's headwear; men's headwear is broken down into caps and hats; hats are broken down into straw hats and felt hats; felt hats break down into bodies, bands, and linings. For each branch of this family tree, there are one or more associations with union contracts." (Carpenter, just cited, p. 38.)

15. Restrictions in the building trades are imposed in most labor markets. However, according to some students of the issue, the total effect on productivity is not very significant. See W. Haber and H. M. Levinson, *Labor Relations and Productivity in the Building Trades* (Ann Arbor, 1956).

16. According to some estimates, multi-employer bargaining covers about one-third of the organized workers in the country; see Neil W. Chamberlain, *Labor* (New York, 1958), p. 161. Our rough estimate suggests that in the New York Metropolitan Region over 40 per cent of the organized workers in manufacturing and a large majority in services and construction are covered by such agreements.

17. See Dunlop (our note 10, above), pp. 33–39. Among the factors which Dunlop considers as impeding the future growth of unionism are: (1) smaller plants scattered over many areas; (2) location of plants in smaller communities and newer areas; (3) scattering of workers in suburbs rather than in neighborhoods close to plants; (4) growing importance of women in the labor force; (5) rise of personnel departments and policies which make union drives more difficult.

18. This has also been the trend in the past. For example, between 1939 and 1953 the fastest growth of union membership was experienced by states which also had the largest percentage increases in nonagricultural employment. See Leo Troy, *Distribution of Union Membership among the States, 1939 and 1953*, National Bureau of Economic Research (New York, 1957), p. 9.

19. For a statement on this situation, see Arthur L. Reuter, Acting Commissioner of Investigation of the State of New York, *Report on the Activities and Associations of Persons Identified as Present . . . at Apalachin, New York, on November 14, 1957, and the Reasons for Their Presence,* mimeo., Apr. 23, 1958, p. 28.

Chapter 3: wages and fringe benefits

1. In women's coats and suits, the high level of Chicago's wages may be partly due to the fact that the area represented is only Cook County, rather than the total metropolitan area of Chicago.

2. This point should not be overemphasized. The latest available survey of occupational wages in men's suits and coats (1951) showed that wages in Chicago, for instance, were about 85 per cent of those in New York—a figure very similar to that of our hourly earnings percentage. For the results of the 1951 survey see "Men's and Boys' Suit and Coat Industry: Earnings, March 1951," *Monthly Labor Review* (November 1951), p. 573.

3. In the textile dyeing and finishing industry, the wage data do not reveal the full labor-cost disadvantage of the Region's producers. These producers in the New York Metropolitan Region are also faced with the fact that workers will not operate as many machines as in other areas. This subject will be further discussed in Chapter 4.

4. Wage surveys conducted by the U. S. Bureau of Labor Statistics indicate that generally—though by no means universally—wage levels in a given section of the country tend to be lower in smaller cities than in the large urban centers of the same section. See Toivo Kanninen, "Wage Differences Among 40 Labor Markets," *Monthly Labor Review* (December 1952), p. 623; also H. M. Douty, "Union and Nonunion Wages," Chapter 43 in W. S. Woytinsky, *Employment and Wages in the United States* (New York: Twentieth Century Fund, 1953), p. 996.

5. See Alfred G. Dale, "Texas' Expansive Clothing Industry," *Texas Business Review,* November 1954.

6. Consider, for example, some wage comparisons in "women's cement process shoes," computed from a 1953 Bureau of Labor Statistics study. If New York City's wages are taken as 100 and if the New York occupational mix is used in the calculations, then Boston's wages appear as 77, but the wages of some towns in Maine appear as 70; similarly, St. Louis' wages are calculated as 77, while the rest of Missouri is 62.

7. For example, such Pennsylvania counties as Lackawanna and Schuylkill (not included in our comparison) attract dress manufacturers from New York because of low labor costs. See Roy B. Helfgott, "Women's and Children's Apparel," in *Made in New York,* ed. Max Hall (Cambridge: Harvard University Press, 1959), especially pp. 84–88.

8. Of the 6,543 workers employed in August 1955 on this type of product in New York, there were 3,682 female sewing machine operators, tailor sys-

tem, and 549 men cutters. Under the tailor system the operator works on the whole garment instead of on only one portion of it, as in the "section system."

9. For example, the New York female sewing machine operator, tailor system, earned on the average 15 cents per hour less in the lowest price line of dresses than in the next higher line. Between the highest and the lowest price line, the difference was 49 cents per hour. See U. S. Bureau of Labor Statistics, *Women's and Misses' Dresses, 1955,* Form OWR-24 for New York, N. Y.

10. If the producers of cheaper lines outside New York City employ primarily the less skilled and lower paid section-system operators, rather than tailor-system operators, the difference may be larger still. Philadelphia, for instance, would rank as a considerably lower wage center for such producers than New York, since lower price lines are produced there largely by section operators. For further points on the problems of the comparison, see Appendix A.

11. Helfgott (note 7, above), p. 85.

12. Computed from Department of Commerce data by the Chamber of Commerce of the United States, *Fringe Benefits—1955* (Washington, 1956), p. 35.

13. Chamber of Commerce, just cited, p. 29.

14. U. S. Bureau of Labor Statistics, *Problems in Measurement of Expenditures on Selected Items of Supplementary Employee Remuneration, January 1956* (Bulletin No. 1186), p. 9.

15. Not including skirts, even though they are often placed in same industry with coats and suits.

16. This and the preceding paragraph are based on Bureau of Labor Statistics surveys of the "men's dress shirts and nightwear" industry (1957) and "men's suits and coats" (1951); on information gathered during field interviews; and on reports in *The Amalgamated Welfare Plan, Biennial Report, 1954-1955,* published by the Amalgamated Clothing Workers of America.

17. For the conditions in the textile dyeing and finishing industry see U. S. Bureau of Labor Statistics, *Wage Structure—Textile Dyeing and Finishing, 1956* (Report No. 110 and Form OWR-24 for Paterson, N. J.).

18. The cost of legally required payments for Social Security, unemployment compensation, and workmen's compensation are not included in these comparisons. Of the three, workmen's compensation is least important as a cost, but displays greatest interregional variation, partly because of variation in state benefit provisions and partly because of differences in methods of administering claims. Available studies of workmen's compensation suggest that New York State generally ranks second after Massachusetts in terms of cost to the employer, though New Jersey and Connecticut do not appear to rate particularly high. In the last six years, as a result of a series of reductions in New York State, the gap between New York State costs and the costs of the states ranking below it has been decreasing. See Associated Industries of New York State, *A Pattern for Progress in Workmen's Compensation* (Albany,

1957), and Joseph Keiper *et al., Studies in Workmen's Compensation* (New York: Commerce and Industry Association of New York, Inc., 1954). Business representatives interviewed during the present study did not consider the levels of workmen's compensation in the Region as a significant locational disadvantage.

19. See James M. Hund, "Electronics," in *Made in New York* (cited in our note 7, above), pp. 286–287.

20. The relatively high wage position of the New York bakery industry is to some extent explained by the great specialization of the production. However, a 1946 study of the Bureau of Labor Statistics, based on occupational earnings of a uniform group of craftsmen, gave results very similar to those revealed in Table 11. See Bureau of Labor Statistics, *Trends in Wage Differentials, 1907–1947* (reprints from *Monthly Labor Review*), p. 10.

21. Other sources indicate that San Francisco is a somewhat higher wage area than Los Angeles. See, for instance, Frank C. Pierson, *Community Wage Patterns* (Berkeley, 1953), p. 170, Table 4–A.

22. See U. S. Bureau of Labor Statistics, *Union Wages and Hours—Book and Job Printing Industry, July 1, 1955* (Bulletin No. 1194).

23. Our own data on the ship building and repairing industry, also to a large extent a local-market industry, show the wages of the Region as being below those of Boston and slightly above those of Philadelphia. For the data on electroplating and on sheet-metal work, see *Monthly Labor Review* (October 1952), p. 45, and *Monthly Labor Review* (August 1952), p. 176.

24. *Monthly Labor Review* (January 1954), p. 45; *Monthly Labor Review* (April 1952), p. 406.

25. Of course, there are also other important reasons for wage variation within a metropolitan area. The establishments in central cities are likely to be larger and to be producing a somewhat different service than those elsewhere. Hotels in Manhattan, for instance, differ from hotels in Jersey City in the service they offer.

26. These are usually termed "private carriers," as distinguished from trucking firms themselves, which are classified as "common" and "contract" carriers. In the sample of the 1955–1956 Bureau of Labor Statistics occupational wage survey of New York, an overwhelming majority of truckdrivers were employed in industries other than the trucking industry. The latter was included, together with telephone, telegraph, electric and gas utilities, in a category designated as "public utilities." This category employed only about one-fourth of the largest category of truckdrivers, those operating medium-size vehicles. See U. S. Bureau of Labor Statistics, *Occupational Wage Survey, New York, New York, April 1956* (Bulletin No. 1188–17).

27. We shall discuss these influences more thoroughly in Chapter 5.

28. For a discussion of this phenomenon see John T. Dunlop, "The Task of Contemporary Wage Theory," in *New Concepts in Wage Determination*, ed. George W. Taylor and Frank C. Pierson (New York, 1957), pp. 134–136.

29. As Table 13 shows, the wages of truckdrivers used here are those in

nonmanufacturing activities. In this sector of a particular area's economy, the local (as distinguished from industrywide) influences on wages are likely to be strongest.

30. They are also higher than wages in Providence, Baltimore, and New Orleans, which are not presented in the table. The relative position of Pittsburgh, as shown in the table, is less clear.

31. In 1953, the Bureau of Labor Statistics made a wage survey of another local service industry—automobile repair shops. The results of this survey show a pattern of wage differences very similar to the one indicated in Table 12. Again, New York and Newark-Jersey City had higher wages than the areas in the East or South. See *Monthly Labor Review* (February 1954), p. 157. Fragmentary comparisons for 1956–1957 in the services given for 1955 in the table show the same general pattern.

32. As we shall indicate in Chapter 5, office workers' salaries vary among broad industrial categories of employment in a well defined and stable pattern of differentials.

33. The salary data for Boston were not available for the 1955–1956 winter period. However, a BLS survey for 1956–1957 did include Boston. The same survey also included an inter-area pay comparison in which salaries in various metropolitan areas were expressed as a percentage of New York City's salaries. For Boston, this comparison was 88 per cent for all three categories—"all industries," "manufacturing," and "nonmanufacturing." See Bureau of Labor Statistics, *Wages and Related Benefits, 17 Labor Markets, 1956–1957* (Bulletin No. 1202), p. 15.

34. See U.S. Bureau of Labor Statistics, just cited, p. 13.

35. Accordingly, in Table 16, New York City's office salaries in manufacturing have been derived from salaries in local plant offices only, since such offices represent the bulk of office employment in manufacturing in other areas. If central offices had been included in the New York City figure, it would have been raised by about 2 per cent, and the ratios of other areas would have been correspondingly lowered. However, New York City and Newark–Jersey City would still occupy fifth and sixth place respectively among the ten areas in Table 16.

36. This industry includes establishments specializing in producing equipment such as printing or packaging machinery. The wages of the relatively small jobbing shops producing machine tools or machine tool accessories for the local market have been largely eliminated from the over-all wage averages used in the comparison. In no two areas is the composition of the machinery industry the same. For example, in Chicago many producers are in the agricultural equipment field, while in New York the dominant establishments are in the printing machinery group. But the basic skills used in a wide variety of machine-building establishments are highly interchangeable among individual specialized plants, and the wages in any particular area are likely to be closely interrelated.

37. As we indicated in Chapter 1, *changes* in wages are frequently uniform

in many companies which maintain different wage *levels* in different labor markets.

38. For a discussion of tendencies toward centralization and uniformity in administration of these benefits, see Helen Baker and Robert R. France, *Centralization and Decentralization in Industrial Relations* (Princeton, N. J., 1954). The findings of a Bureau of Labor Statistics study also suggest that pension or insurance plans are likely to be administered in a multiplant firm on a companywide basis. See Bureau of Labor Statistics, *Problems in Measurement of Expenditures on Selected Items of Supplementary Employee Remuneration* (Bulletin No. 1186), p. 16.

39. The very fact that it is difficult to make interregional comparisons in this field reduces the importance of such comparisons as a locational force. Prospective employers, considering whether or not to locate in one area as compared with another, can make comparisons only to the extent that the data exist to make them.

Chapter 4: postwar trends in wages

1. See John O. Tomb, "Should Industry Move South," *Harvard Business Review* (September–October 1953), pp. 83–90; also George H. Hildebrand, "The Economic Effects of Unionism," in *A Decade of Industrial Relations Research 1946–1956*, ed. Neil W. Chamberlain, Frank C. Pierson, Theresa Wolfson (New York, 1958), p. 126, and literature cited therein.

2. Willis D. Weatherford, Jr., *Geographic Differentials of Agricultural Wages in the United States* (Cambridge, Mass., 1957), p. 16.

3. Some narrowing of wage differences was also evident in other industries not shown in Table 21—for example, children's dresses and men's dress shirts. However, it is important to note that our comparison does *not* include smaller communities of New England, Pennsylvania, or any of the southern states. This point will be further emphasized in a later section of the chapter.

4. Unfortunately the comparison of office workers' salaries had to be limited to only a few metropolitan areas; no comparison for this period was possible for most of the important areas because of lack of data.

5. Because of the use of average hourly earnings, which reflect also differences in the skill composition of the work force, the national average in the women's and misses' dresses industry appears very low in comparison with the Region's wages. But the relative change in the levels of hourly earnings in the nation and in the Region, shown in Table 23, is generally consistent with wage statistics for the 1947–1955 period which are based on an earnings index of a fixed group of occupations in a number of metropolitan areas.

6. U. S. Department of Commerce and Labor, *Bulletin of the Bureau of Labor*, No. 77 (July 1908), Table IV, pp. 133–162.

7. Even in that period small communities had much lower wages than large cities. See Paul H. Douglas, *Real Wages in the United States* (Boston and New York, 1930), p. 189.

8. I. A. Hourwich, *Immigration and Labor* (New York, 1922), p. 372.

9. Reports of the Immigration Commission, *Immigrants in Industries,* 61st Cong., S. Doc. 633 (Washington, 1911), p. 380.

10. Carter Goodrich *et al., Migration and Economic Opportunity* (Philadelphia, 1936), pp. 676–683; U. S. Department of Commerce, *Long-Term Regional Trends in Manufacturing Growth, 1899–1955,* Area Trend Series No. 2 (February 1956), pp. 4–5; *Monthly Labor Review* (July 1950), p. 108; Lloyd G. Reynolds, *Labor Economics and Labor Relations* (New York, 1954), p. 503.

11. Theodore W. Schultz, *Agriculture in an Unstable Economy* (New York, 1945), p. 105.

12. Lloyd G. Reynolds and Cynthia H. Taft, *The Evolution of Wage Structure* (New Haven, 1956), p. 181; Weatherford (our note 2, above), p. 61.

13. Weatherford (our note 2, above), p. 81. Also see Reynolds and Taft, p. 182; Hildebrand (note 1, above), p. 126. However, migration of labor has undoubtedly contributed to the narrowing of wages and incomes between the Pacific Coast and the rest of the nation. Compare Seymour Harris, "Interregional Competition," *American Economic Review, Papers and Proceedings* (May 1954), p. 374.

14. Lloyd G. Reynolds, *The Structure of Labor Markets* (New York, 1951), p. 242; H. Makower, J. Marshak, and H. W. Robinson, "Studies in the Mobility of Labor," *Oxford Economic Papers* (October 1938, May 1939, September 1940); Weatherford, p. 61.

15. Reynolds, *Structure of Labor Markets,* pp. 226, 246.

16. The experience of 1943–1945 is well analyzed in Nedra B. Belloc, *Wages in California* (Berkeley and Los Angeles, 1948), pp. 66–71.

17. The emphasis on soft-goods industries in the existing industrial composition of the southern states handicapped those states in obtaining their share of wartime industrial expansion. See U. S. Department of Commerce, *Long-Term Regional Trends in Manufacturing Growth, 1899–1955,* Area Trend Series No. 2 (February 1956), p. 10.

18. In fact, in the postwar period, employment opportunities have been expanding at a faster rate in the South and other less industrialized areas than in the industrialized areas of the Northeast or Midwest. U. S. Department of Commerce, just cited, p. 8.

19. For an extended discussion of the concept of "secondary labor force" see Richard C. Wilcock, "The Secondary Labor Force and the Measurement of Unemployment," in National Bureau of Economic Research, *The Measurement and Behavior of Unemployment* (Princeton, N. J., 1957), pp. 167–178.

20. Richard C. Wilcock and Irvin Sobel, "Secondary Labor Force Mobility in Four Midwestern Shoe Towns," *Industrial and Labor Relations Review* (July 1955), pp. 527, 539.

21. *Ibid.,* p. 535.

22. Edgar M. Hoover, *The Location of Economic Activity* (New York, 1948), p. 196.

23. A. J. Jaffe, "Demographic and Labor Force Characteristics of the New

York City Puerto Rican Population," in Bureau of Applied Social Research, Columbia University, *Puerto Rican Population of New York City* (New York, 1954), p. 25.

24. A detailed analysis of these developments will be found in another volume in the New York Metropolitan Region Study: Benjamin Chinitz's *Freight and the Metropolis.* See also U. S. Department of Commerce (our note 17, above), p. 9.

25. Hildebrand (note 1, above), p. 126.

26. It should be recognized that wages in the South are low partly because of the relative predominance of industries which, even on a national scale, are relatively low-paying. This fact creates an environment in which the general community wage levels are further pulled down by the industrial composition of the areas. Partly, but only partly, because of this, the relatively high wage industries also pay lower wages in the low income areas of the South than in other markets. See Frank A. Hanna, "Analysis of Interstate Income Differentials," and the discussion accompanying the paper, in *Regional Income,* which is Vol. 21 of National Bureau of Economic Research, *Studies in Income and Wealth* (Princeton, N. J., 1957). pp. 113–193.

27. "Effects of the $1 Minimum Wage: Men's and Boys' Shirt Industry," *Monthly Labor Review* (November 1957), p. 1339.

28. U. S. Bureau of Labor Statistics, *Textile Dyeing and Finishing, 1946* (Wage Structure, Series 2, No. 44), p. 1; BLS, *Textile Dyeing and Finishing, April 1956* (Report No. 110).

29. U. S. Department of Labor, Wage and Hour and Public Contracts Division, *Studies of the Economic Effects of the $1.00 Minimum Wage* (March 1957).

30. Compare Clark Kerr, "Wage Relationships—The Comparative Impact of Market and Power Forces," in *The Theory of Wage Determination,* ed. John T. Dunlop (London, 1957), p. 186.

31. Wage increases in the local transit industry frequently lead to fare rises. Under such conditions strong justification is needed for a wage increase and no other local industry provides a completely suitable standard. A union argument based largely on a comparison of wages in other areas is reproduced in John T. Dunlop and J. J. Healy, *Collective Bargaining* (Homewood, Ill., 1954), pp. 361–378.

32. A careful study showed that wages of hotel workers in unionized areas increased more than those in nonunion cities. See Joseph Scherer, "The Union Impact on Wages: The Case of the Year-round Hotel Industry," *Industrial and Labor Relations Review* (January 1956), pp. 213–224.

33. We suspect that, if we could include benefits in the 1955 outlays, the same results would be obtained in the power laundry industry, which also shows a reduction of wage differences. As we observed in the preceding chapter, New York employers in this service, unlike those in other cities, generally provide the workers with a union-negotiated pension plan.

34. See Roy B. Helfgott's study of the women's apparel industries in an-

other volume in this series, *Made in New York*, ed. Max Hall (Cambridge: Harvard University Press, 1959), p. 89.

35. The influence of unionism is hard to isolate. We must note that wages have been rising in the other industries of these areas more rapidly than in the garment trades. Moreover, Puerto Ricans were not available generally outside the Region. Unionism has been, at best, only one factor in reducing differences between the Region and other areas.

36. Leo Wolman, *Ebb and Flow in Trade Unionism* (New York, 1936), p. 86.

37. Helfgott (note 34, above), p. 85.

38. The description in the preceding paragraphs is based on our field interviews. But the 1958 strike of the International Ladies' Garment Workers' Union in the shops of New York, New Jersey, and Pennsylvania, which took place several months after our field work was completed, confirmed the importance of the problem of maintenance of contract standards. A breakdown in the maintenance of contract standards was a major factor in precipitating the strike. Similarly, Roy B. Helfgott's special study of the women's garment industry, made for the New York Metropolitan Region Study (our note 34, above), confirms the picture presented here. See his pp. 90–92.

39. For a discussion of the problem of intra-union competition in the dress industry in the period before World War II, see Leonard A. Drake and Carrie Glasser, *Trends in the New York Clothing Industry* (New York, 1942), p. 123.

40. "The Amalgamated had an internal explosion to worry about this afternoon . . . and conflict between delegates from New York and other clothing centers over a breakdown of industrial liberty almost caused a fist fight on the convention floor. The disorder broke out after Abe Chatman, manager of the Rochester Joint Board, had belittled New York complaints that contract standards were being violated in other areas, thus jeopardizing New York jobs. The row made it plain that the Amalgamated was beset with stabilization problems akin to those that have afflicted its sister union, the ILGWU." ("U. S. to Aid Unions in Buying Clothes," *New York Times*, May 16, 1958.) This story confirmed the results of our field interviews.

41. The calculations were based on data chosen from Bureau of Labor Statistics, *Women's and Misses Dresses 1955*, Forms OWR–24 for Dallas and Wilkes-Barre. We first calculated the effect of increases up to $1 of those workers who were getting less than the minimum wage. Then we also added an increase which would be a result of an indirect impact of the minimum wage change. In estimating the indirect impact we were more "generous" to the workers than the available data on the past minimum changes would justify. This indirect impact we considered to be of a magnitude of 200 per cent of the direct effect. This is a much greater indirect impact than any recorded previously. For instance, in 1950 the indirect impact of the 75-cent minimum was 64 per cent of the direct effect in the work clothing industry; in the "single pants" industry it was 17 per cent. For a discussion of the indirect im-

pact see Harry Weiss, "Economic Effects of a Nationwide Minimum Wage," in *Industrial Relations Research Association, Papers Presented at Cleveland, Ohio, 1956*, p. 159.

42. For example, even in August 1948—a year and a half before the 1950 minimum—only the janitors and packers were receiving less than one dollar per hour in Baltimore, the lowest wage labor market in men's suits and coats which was studied by the Bureau of Labor Statistics. However, no wage data are available for smaller communities in which only one or two plants may be located. See *Monthly Labor Review* (February 1949), p. 190.

43. John M. Peterson, "Employment Effects of Minimum Wages 1938–50," *Journal of Political Economy* (October 1957), p. 423.

44. Weiss (note 41, above), p. 160.

45. See Bureau of Labor Statistics, *Wage Structure, Men's Dress Shirts and Nightwear, 1950* (Series 2, No. 80); BLS, *Wage Structure, Men's and Boys' Dress Shirts and Nightwear, May 1954* (Report No. 74).

46. "Effects of the $1 Minimum Wage: Men's and Boy's Shirt Industry," *Monthly Labor Review* (November 1957), p. 1341.

47. E. R. Livernash, "Collective Bargaining and Competitive Cost in the Shoe Industry," *Monthly Labor Review* (November 1957), pp. 310–322.

48. This reduction is shown in Table 23, in which the Region's wages were compared with the national averages.

Chapter 5: pressures from within the region

1. Melvin W. Reder, "The Theory of Union Wage Policy," *Review of Economics and Statistics* (February 1952), p. 37. See also Carl M. Stevens, "On the Theory of Negotiation," *Quarterly Journal of Economics* (February 1958), p. 89.

2. Sumner H. Slichter, "Notes on the Structure of Wages," *Review of Economics and Statistics* (February 1950), pp. 80–91; Lloyd G. Reynolds, *The Structure of Labor Markets* (New York, 1951), p. 187; John T. Dunlop, "The Task of Contemporary Wage Theory," in *New Concepts in Wage Determination*, ed. George W. Taylor and Frank C. Pierson (New York, 1957), p. 135.

3. Dunlop, just cited, p. 136; Melvin W. Reder, "Wage Determination in Theory and Practice," in *A Decade of Industrial Relations Research, 1946–1956*, ed. Neil W. Chamberlain, Frank C. Pierson, Theresa Wolfson (New York, 1958), pp. 72–73.

4. Reder (see note 3, above), p. 73; George Seltzer, "Pattern Bargaining and the United Steelworkers," *Journal of Political Economy* (August 1951). In the New York Region the negotiated rates for assembly workers in electronic component plants are about 10 cents lower than in television plants, organized by the same union.

5. Reynolds, p. 158; Dunlop, p. 138 (both cited in our note 2, above).

6. Reynolds, p. 220.

7. Reynolds, p. 161.

8. See Will Herberg, "The Old-Timers and the Newcomers: Ethnic Group Relations in a Needle Trade Union," *Journal of Social Issues*, 9:12–29 (1953). Examining the ethnic composition of a dressmakers' local, Herberg shows that between 1934 and 1953 the proportion of Negroes and Puerto Rican members increased from 16 to 32 per cent. The figures for new members are more striking. Already in 1948, Latin Americans and Negroes constituted half of the new members joining the local union. See also Roy B. Helfgott, "Puerto Rican Integration in a Garment Union Local," in *Industrial Relations Research Association, Papers Presented at New York City, 1957*, pp. 269–275.

9. The concern of these garment representatives seems well justified in the light of some of the available data on the age distribution of the work force in at least one industry. A 1954 tabulation of the age distribution of membership of eight locals organizing the work force in women's coats, suits, and skirts showed that 60 per cent of the workers were 50 years old or over, and 30 per cent were 60 years old or over. Data for 1958 for some of the same locals show an even more striking picture of age distribution. For example, in the New York City local of sewing machine operators, more than 50 per cent of the members were 61 years old or more. Data supplied by the Joint Board of Cloak, Suit, Skirt and Reefer Makers' Union of Greater New York (ILGWU).

10. Between 1947 and 1956, the proportion of Puerto Rican immigrants to the continent who have settled in New York decreased from 95 to 65 per cent. (*Bulletin*, Department of City Planning, New York City, February 1957.) This striking change in the geographical distribution of the immigrants reflects, we believe, the fact that the relatively limited employment opportunities for male labor in New York have been an important factor in restricting the number of Puerto Ricans who settle in the Region.

11. A. J. Jaffe, "Demographic and Labor Force Characteristics of the New York City Puerto Rican Population," in Bureau of Applied Social Research, Columbia University, *Puerto Rican Population of New York City* (New York, 1954), p. 10.

12. The lag in the increase of wages of the garment industries is only slightly associated with the original wage level of the industries in 1947. If we divide the industries into separate groups on the basis of the absolute wage level in 1947, the garment industries' wage increase is still about half or less of the increase in other industries in each wage group. Within the garment sector, however, some of the largest percentage increases were in the industries which had relatively low wages in 1947.

13. For several industries which employ Puerto Ricans and Negroes and which were listed earlier, no wage data are available for the 1947–1955 period.

14. In 23 of the 28 industries, wages increased more slowly in New York City than in the rest of the Region.

15. These figures represent employees covered by unemployment compensation, derived from tabulations for the 22 counties of the Region. The tabulations were obtained from the labor departments of New York State, New

Jersey, and Connecticut, adjusted in some instances by New York Metropolitan Region Study.

16. The impact of space considerations on industrial location is analyzed in detail in Edgar M. Hoover and Raymond Vernon, *Anatomy of a Metropolis* (Cambridge: Harvard University Press, 1959), especially pp. 29–36.

17. Search for space and changes in transport technology are not the only forces underlying the outward movement of manufacturing in the Region. For example, petroleum refineries and chemical plants—the so-called "nuisance" industries—moved decades ago to the edges of the heaviest population masses because of residential expansion in their previous locations in Manhattan and Brooklyn.

18. Between 1947 and 1956, New York City's share of the Region's employment in plants having 121 and more workers declined by 18 per cent; plants having 61 to 120 workers by 8.5 per cent; and in plants having 60 workers or less by 6 per cent. (Computed from data supplied by departments of labor of New York State, New Jersey, and Connecticut.)

CHAPTER 6: THE WAGE FACTOR AND THE REGION'S FUTURE

1. Leonard A. Drake and Carrie Glasser, *Trends in the New York Clothing Industry* (New York, 1942), p. 42.

2. The following paragraphs are based on: Lucy W. Killough, "The Tobacco Products Industry," in *Regional Survey of New York and Its Environs,* Vol. IA (New York, 1928); Russell H. Mack, *Factors of Instability Affecting Production and Employment in the Cigar Manufacturing Industry* (Philadelphia, 1933); L. Earl Lewis, "Earnings in Cigar Manufacturing," *Monthly Labor Review,* December 1955.

3. The sketch of shifts in garment industries is based to a large extent on Drake and Glasser (note 1, above); B. M. Selekman, H. R. Walter, W. J. Couper, "The Clothing and Textile Industries," in *Regional Survey of New York and Its Environs,* Vol. IB (New York, 1928); Roy B. Helfgott, "Women's and Children's Apparel" in *Made in New York,* ed. Max Hall (Cambridge: Harvard University Press, 1959).

4. Drake and Glasser, p. 109; Mabel A. Magee, *Trends in Location of the Women's Clothing Industry* (Chicago, 1930), p. 45. There are several factors which contributed to New York's emergence as a high wage area. In the past, New York's garment trades relied on immigrant labor to a greater extent than the same industries in other areas. Even though the influx of immigrants stopped and many Jewish women were leaving the labor force, New York City still experienced a rapid growth of garment trades—particularly in the most expensive lines where wages were highest. What is more, the unions in New York were stronger than in most other areas. In later years New York's wages in men's clothing exceeded those of Chicago. Data showing the relatively heavy reliance of New York garment trades on immigrants are in *Reports of the Industrial Commission on Immigration,* Vol. 15 (Washington, 1901), p. 319.

5. Leonard A. Drake, *Trends in the New York Printing Industry* (New York, 1940), p. 56.

6. Drake, just cited, p. 61; W. Eric Gustafson, "Printing and Publishing," in *Made in New York* (note 3, above).

7. There are some minor differences between the classifications used in this chapter for measuring trends and those used in Table 3 of Chapter 1. In this chapter, the classification as between national and local industries is made on the basis of the industry's locational characteristics in the nation as a whole rather than on its characteristics specifically in the New York area.

8. New York City also showed some decline in the medium price lines. But in the main this was probably caused by the shifting of production from the City to other counties of the Region. See Helfgott, cited in note 3, above.

9. The influence of the industrial mix is thoroughly analyzed by Robert M. Lichtenberg (see note on page 149).

10. *Regional Survey,* Vol. IA (see our note 2, above), p. 36.

Index

Bei Fragen zur Produktsicherheit wenden Sie sich bitte an:
If you have any questions regarding product safety,
please contact:

Walter de Gruyter GmbH
Genthiner Straße 13
10785 Berlin
productsafety@degruyterbrill.com